Strategic Options for Bush Administration Climate Policy

Lee Lane

The AEI Press

Publisher for the American Enterprise Institute

WASHINGTON, D.C.

2006

Distributed to the Trade by National Book Network, 15200 NBN Way, Blue Ridge Summit, PA 17214. To order call toll free 1-800-462-6420 or 1-717-794-3800. For all other inquiries please contact the AEI Press, 1150 Seventeenth Street, N.W., Washington, D.C. 20036 or call 1-800-862-5801.

Library of Congress Cataloging-in-Publication Data
Lane, Lee.
   Strategic options for Bush administration climate policy / by Lee Lane.
      p. cm.
Includes bibliographical references.
   ISBN-13: 978-0-8447-7196-0 (pbk : alk. paper)
   ISBN-10: 0-8447-7196-1
   1. Climatic changes—Government policy—United States. 2. Environmental policy—United States. I. Title.

   QC981.8.C5L365 2006
   363.738'745610973--dc22

                                              2006034270

  11 10 09 08 07 06   1 2 3 4 5 6

Printed in the United States of America

Contents

Acknowledgments

Many people contributed to producing this book. The project would have been impossible without the efforts of AEI's Sam Thernstrom, who supported it despite intense demands of other work and the task of welcoming home a new member of the Thernstrom family. Sam's copy editor, Lisa Ferraro Parmelee, also performed admirably under difficult circumstances and unusual time pressure. Valerie Bredy of the Climate Policy Center played a vital role at every stage of the work. Charlie Coggeshall did an excellent job of actually finding all those references that "I remembered reading somewhere."

I am particularly grateful to my numerous reviewers, including Dick van Atta, Dave Conover, Brian Dick, William Fulkerson, Chris Green, Dave Van Hoogstraten, Bob Marlay, Robert Means, Bill O'Keefe, Rafe Pomerance, Anne Smith, and Trigg Talley. Each made valuable contributions. Any remaining mistakes and deficiencies are solely my responsibility.

Introduction

The philosopher Wilhelm Dilthey believed that historians who judge past events by the standards of later eras are acting ahistorically and arbitrarily. It was more valid and illuminating, he suggested, to ask whether earlier statesmen's actions were internally consistent and well-aligned with existing circumstances, an approach that he called "immanent critique."[1]

In judging contemporary climate policies, some scientists and environmental activists resemble the historians of whom Dilthey complained. They ignore the government's own priorities, its constraints, and the broader political context in which climate policy is formulated. Judged by such unworldly standards, no actual governmental climate policy is likely to win approval.

In assessing the Bush administration's climate policy options and choices, this book adopts an approach akin to Dilthey's immanent critique. It asks how well the administration's climate policies serve the president's stated goals and how well they conform to the larger political and economic framework that shapes and constrains his actions. In its course, it will also evaluate the critiques of administration policies often heard from environmentalists.

To conduct this kind of inquiry one must first identify the administration's climate policy goals. I believe President Bush has five climate policy objectives: 1) increasing knowledge of climate change science; 2) reducing greenhouse gas emissions now; 3) developing clean energy technologies that will enable us to make cost-effective emissions reductions in the future; 4) promoting cooperative international efforts to address climate change, especially in the developing world; while 5) protecting the American economy.

1

It is also necessary to know something of the circumstances shaping and constraining the administration's climate policy. Some of these factors are known only to the administration itself, but the most important constraints are transparent. The science of climate change and the economics of greenhouse gas abatement eliminate many policy options. A less obvious, but no less important, factor is that political and economic institutions (and sometimes the absence of them) sharply curtail the range of possible climate policy choices.

Nobel laureate economic historian Douglas North explains that institutions channel and limit human action.[2] Viewing climate policy through an institutional prism suggests three hypotheses.[3] First, the absence of international institutions for third-party enforcement of agreements makes the fashioning of broad and effective international greenhouse gas controls difficult or impossible. Second, the dynamics of domestic political institutions often seriously compromise the cost-effectiveness of real-world climate policies. Third, today's policy choices, especially those that set new "rules of the climate policy game," will enduringly shape and limit tomorrow's policy options.

To some critics of the Bush administration, this framework will seem needlessly complex. To them, the right direction for climate policy seems self-evident. Stopping climate change presents, in their view, a pollution-control problem. Eliminating the anthropogenic (manmade) greenhouse gas (GHG) emissions that cause or at least contribute to climate change will require a mandatory system of international controls such as the Kyoto Protocol. They believe the Bush administration is culpable for withdrawing from the protocol, and that it should make amends by either adhering to Kyoto or proposing an alternative to it.

This critique ignores fundamental distinctions between climate change and conventional pollution problems. Without third-party institutions to enforce participation and compliance in international controls, the high costs of GHG abatement ensure that agreements like the Kyoto Protocol are bound to fail. And without a sufficiently inclusive and effective international control regime, domestic controls can accomplish virtually nothing.

This reasoning will be explored in more detail in the following pages. By way of introduction, the reader might consider one question: Is there any historical precedent for a successful international agreement with the characteristics that would be required for a successful international GHG control regime?

Those characteristics include the following:

- Forty or so disparate nations (the major emitters) must negotiate an agreement that would require all of them to incur significant economic costs and social disruption.

- Benefits would be uncertain, long-deferred, and hard to measure.

- Every year, every participant could gain economically by either cheating or exiting the agreement altogether. If exit or cheating became more than marginal, international economic competition would cause the entire agreement to unravel. To forestall this outcome, a few nations would not only have to pay abatement costs; they would also have to bear the costs of enforcing the agreement on the environmentally less punctilious.

- The agreement must function effectively for at least a century.

- And, as developing country economies grow to the point where their emissions become significant, those countries must be persuaded to join the agreement as well, at just the time when their economies are beginning to bear their greatest fruit.

One could cite additional complicating factors. Some countries, whose participation in an agreement would be essential, are rivals in regional power struggles. (The United States and China are obvious examples, but there are many others.) Some national governments lack the domestic consensus (and political legitimacy) required to impose the necessary sacrifices on their own populations. (China and India probably both fit in this category.) Countries differ a lot in the degree to which climate change threatens them, greatly complicating the search for international consensus. Presumably, the basic point is already plain: Successful international cooperation on a problem that remotely approaches the difficulty level entailed by GHG controls would be unprecedented.

Considering these difficulties, it is hard not to suspect that attempts to construct international GHG control regimes like Kyoto are simply quixotic. If so, by discarding the protocol, President Bush extricated the United States from a policy dead end. Exiting Kyoto spared America high costs in pursuit of a hopeless cause. By inference, much of the environmentalist critique of Bush administration climate policy stands on unsound foundations.

The administration's emphasis on climate-related research and development (R&D) is also potentially fruitful. As already noted, high abatement costs are a major deterrent to international adoption of GHG controls. And drastically lower abatement costs would be a necessary condition—although not a sufficient one—for someday constructing a successful international GHG control regime. R&D might also produce innovative countermeasures that could obviate the need for expensive GHG abatement.

Despite its virtues, Bush administration climate policy runs the risk of failing. Its prospects for significantly reducing the future costs of climate change to a large extent hinge on the administration's climate-related R&D program, called the Climate Change Technology Program (CCTP). Yet CCTP's implementation is plagued by organizational problems and resource scarcity. Defective implementation can undermine the value of having the right goal.

The prospects of avoiding needlessly costly abatement policies are hardly better than those for solving the problem of climate change. The administration appears to be trying to foreclose the possibility of a future American return to the costly and inefficient Kyoto system, a worthy goal. To accomplish it, the president needs alternative international institutions—and public understanding of their advantages over the Kyoto approach. While the Asia-Pacific Partnership holds some promise, a more comprehensive framework is required to deprive cap-and-trade initiatives of their short-term political momentum. What is sometimes referred to as a bottom-up "pledge and review" system could offer a solution. The administration has so far ignored such proposals.

Domestically, the situation is similar. Because *effective* international GHG limits are so unlikely, American GHG controls at this time would be largely an exercise in symbolic politics. Yet most informed political observers agree that mandatory domestic GHG controls are inevitable, although their shape and timing are yet to be determined. The challenge is, therefore, to devise an effective symbolic policy with as little net cost as possible or, optimistically, a small net gain. States are acting already, and Congress cannot be that far behind. Can these well-meaning efforts be crafted so that, at a minimum, they do no harm?

While the Bush administration has done reasonably well in limiting abatement costs on its own watch, it has failed to institutionalize policies that can lastingly impede implementation of Kyoto-style controls. In fact, Kyoto-style policies are gaining ground politically and may well be enacted in the next presidential administration. Ultimately, then, if only for defensive reasons, the Bush administration should consider devising and proposing an expanded climate policy initiative that might succeed in foreclosing the Kyoto-style options that are becoming increasingly popular.

Time is short. Presidential backing would be essential for the prospects of such an initiative. Unless the Bush administration acts decisively, the next administration is likely to shape U.S. climate policy for decades to come. Currently, post-Bush climate policy threatens to become an exercise in needlessly expensive symbolic politics. Leaving an institutional vacuum in U.S. climate policy is an invitation to policy mischief in the coming years.

To avoid this outcome, the administration needs to conduct a rapid review of its climate policy options. Such a review would require strengthening the currently weak institutional base of the executive branch's climate policy process. Substantively, the administration should consider reorganizing its climate-related R&D program and expanding its scope, initiating a new international negotiation designed to boost total global efforts on such R&D, and proposing a modest and carefully structured carbon tax.

1

The Bush Administration
and the Kyoto Protocol

In the Kyoto Protocol, President Bush inherited a poisoned legacy. Implementing the Kyoto Protocol would have significantly harmed the U.S. economy. Entry into this agreement would have offered only trivial environmental benefits. In fact, although expensive, American participation in the agreement would have accomplished little of substance. With American participation or without it, the Kyoto Protocol is largely symbolic.[1] The agreement was so unpopular that the Clinton administration never submitted it to the Senate for ratification—though this has not deterred former president Clinton from criticizing the Bush administration's failure to implement the pact.

In 2001, President Bush rejected the Kyoto Protocol. Notwithstanding this rejection, the protocol survives, and it presents multiple problems for the United States. It impedes the emergence of better international climate policy, and it serves as a rallying cry for anti-American politicians. As a negotiating process, Kyoto's prospects remain murky. As a solution to the problem of climate change, Kyoto is visibly bankrupt.

To deal with the lingering political threat posed by Kyoto, the administration has constructed an alternative international climate policy. The Asia-Pacific Partnership (APP) is its centerpiece. The effectiveness of this policy will depend heavily on whether it can achieve targeted institutional change in China and India. The Global Nuclear Energy Partnership, while propelled largely by nonclimate concerns, may also hold potential for climate policy gains.

The Kyoto Protocol and American National Interest

Since the end of World War II, America has led efforts to develop international arrangements to provide global public goods by massively subsidizing, for instance, military security and peacekeeping. Leadership in developing liberal economic institutions, including the World Trade Organization (WTO), the Group of Eight (G8), the International Monetary Fund (IMF), and the World Bank, are other examples.[2] Indeed, one analysis has recently argued that the United States serves as a sort of informal global government.[3]

American subsidies to these global public goods were not altruistically motivated. Had they been, the domestic political consensus needed to support America's large and sustained investments would long since have collapsed. In fact, the United States gains mightily, both economically and in security, from maintaining international security systems and liberal international institutions.[4] Historically, durable empires and hegemonies have been based on the relatively efficient supply of security, governance, property rights enforcement, and common language. Efficient supply of these public goods benefits both the metropolis and periphery of the empire.[5]

With the Kyoto Protocol, the Clinton administration sought to assert America's leadership in providing another global public good: protection from harmful climate change. The protocol, however, dismally failed the self-interest test. It did not generate net benefits for the United States; indeed, it would have imposed significant net costs on the United States.

The Energy Modeling Forum, which organized a multimodel assessment of Kyoto's likely impact on the American economy, found that the Kyoto Protocol would have reduced the gross domestic product (GDP) of the United States by 0.24 to 1.03 percent by 2010.[6] The mean result of the eight models was a GDP reduction of 0.59 percent.[7] Of course, Kyoto proponents maintain that the agreement's environmental benefits would offset these economic sacrifices.

But, in fact, Kyoto's environmental benefits would have been minuscule. Even with American participation, the protocol would have scarcely affected carbon dioxide (CO_2) concentrations or global warming.[8] In fact, had the original Kyoto agreement (with the United States taking part) become permanent, it would have diminished global mean temperatures by only 0.03°C.[9]

The predictable result of this pattern of significant costs and trivial benefits would have been net costs. Analysis bears out this prediction. For example, with Annex I trading, the Kyoto Protocol would have imposed a present-value net loss of $313 billion (in 1990 dollars) on the United States.[10]

America would have borne a grossly disproportionate share of Kyoto's costs. True, the pre-Marrakech Kyoto Protocol imposed net costs for the world as a whole. One estimate placed the global net losses at $121 billion (again, in 1990 dollars). The estimated benefit–cost ratio was 0.44.[11] However, *excluding the United States*, the world as a whole would have realized net benefits of $108 billion.[12] The Kyoto Protocol's system of compulsory international transfer payments explains this seeming paradox.

International transfer payments from the United States, not environmental benefits, would have been the main source of the rest of the world's net gains. The protocol confers a large stock of bogus emission rights upon the countries of the former Soviet Union (FSU). These allowances are colloquially termed "hot air"; they represent emissions reductions that have *already occurred* since the collapse of the Soviet economy. The Kyoto system would have compelled American businesses to purchase large numbers of hot-air allowances from the FSU. The resulting income transfers would have produced no environmental benefit, but they would have made the FSU nations major net beneficiaries of the agreement.[13]

Kyoto's apologists contend that the Bush administration should have tried to correct the Kyoto Protocol instead of abandoning it. (And, indeed, fixing Kyoto to make it politically viable in the United States was allegedly a goal of the Clinton administration, although the administration never made any serious effort to do so.) Proposals to repair Kyoto must face several troubling facts, however. The first such "inconvenient truth" (to borrow Al Gore's term) is that the agreement's very structure is inimical to American national interests.

Kyoto is based on setting quantitative emission caps (sometimes called hard caps). Kyoto's emission limits are defined in terms of historical (1990) emissions. Any such system necessarily disadvantages high-growth economies. Kyoto's cap-and-trade mechanism required countries with high economic growth rates (and hence significant GHG emission growth) either to incur exorbitant abatement costs or to purchase hot-air emission allowances abroad.

Because the American economy grew rapidly during the 1990s, GHG emissions also rose significantly. Consequently, by the time President Bush took office, the United States would have had to cut GHG emissions by over 30 percent to meet its Kyoto target. It would have had only about a decade to make these reductions—a Herculean task.

In this regard (as in others), the Kyoto Protocol seems unrealistic on its face. It would be hard to imagine a worse model for GHG controls than one imposing arbitrary, quantitative short-term emission caps in a narrow geographic area. Yet Kyoto assumed just this form.

Part of the explanation for Kyoto's poor design may be that the protocol is based more on symbolism than on substance. Symbolic diplomacy is hardly new. Consider the Kellogg-Briand Pact, an agreement among all of the major powers to renounce war that came into effect only about a decade before the outbreak of World War II. An eminent diplomatic historian offered the following assessment:

> The . . . [Kellogg-Briand Pact] was no more than a declaration of intent divorced from any enforcing agency or means; . . . in retrospect it may appear quite futile, as in fact it was destined to be, and, under the best interpretation, the expression of naïveté that may seem difficult of understanding. To the enforcement of peace the Kellogg-Briand Pact contributed nothing but it is a perfect expression and symbol of the widespread atmosphere of 1928. Briand characterized it as a date in the history of mankind, a view to which many at the time would have subscribed.[14]

Among European governments and climate policy enthusiasts, the atmosphere of 2005 (the year of Kyoto ratification) resembled that which Albrecht-Carrie describes as prevailing in 1928. Nations had pledged themselves to virtue—while assiduously avoiding any acknowledgment that the pledges were meaningless. No country was planning war in 1928, so the Kellogg-Briand Pact occasioned few qualms at first. Its vacuity became visible only later, when some countries decided that their interests impelled the outbreak of hostilities.

Kyoto may develop similar compliance problems over time. Its enforcement provisions are certainly feeble: Countries that exceed their targets are subject to penalties in the next commitment period. But nothing compels them to participate in the next commitment period—if there even is one—and it is certainly possible that they could make their continued participation conditional upon a waiver for their previous penalties. If the combined cost of a country's new cap and its penalties from the previous commitment period are too expensive, a country can simply withdraw from the Kyoto system. Domestic political pressure may induce countries to participate in such a system now; the politics of participation may also change in time as costs of compliance mount. In any case, the international system itself does not strengthen the incentive for compliance.

Kyoto's bigger problem, though, is enforcing participation.[15] Thus, most "participants" have refused to accept mandatory emission reduction targets. The United States and Australia simply decline to participate. Far from suffering for their decision, holdouts score automatic economic gains vis-à-vis participants.

Meanwhile, most signatories are not fulfilling their commitments. The European Union (EU) may still reach its Kyoto goals, if it is willing to buy enough bogus emission rights from the FSU (or elsewhere)—but this would have no actual environmental benefit. And Germany and the United Kingdom, where factors other than climate policy have had a large impact on emissions, still account for almost 96 percent of the reductions achieved so far.[16] Ten of fifteen EU members are currently not on course to meet their Kyoto targets.

Elsewhere, prospects for Kyoto's effectiveness are still bleaker. Neither Japan nor Canada seems likely to meet its target. Canada's new government has openly admitted the impossibility and has announced it intends to produce a "made-in-Canada" climate policy independent of Kyoto, although it has not (as of this writing) announced the content of that policy.[17] Russia is openly dismissive of climate change. In the words of British Prime Minister Tony Blair, "The truth is that no country is going to cut its growth or consumption substantially in light of a long-term environmental problem."[18]

Yet the Kyoto Protocol's structure virtually guarantees conflicts with growth. Its architecture combines hard (quantitative) emission caps with aggressive short-term emission reduction goals. To some, this feature testifies to the protocol's unsullied environmental virtue. But it drastically degrades the Kyoto system's cost-effectiveness.

Hard caps are poor climate policy for several reasons. First, from a political standpoint, hard (purely quantitative) caps discourage the explicit comparison of costs and benefits. Compared to price-based policies, quantitative targets allow cap-and-trade proponents to claim that aggressive caps can be met cheaply. By the time society discovers that these claims are false, the legislation is already in place, and changing it is difficult. This gambit raises the odds that countries will adopt inefficiently stringent targets. In private, lobbyists for environmental pressure groups have explicitly told me that they prefer hard caps for this reason. The cumulative costs of attempting excessively deep emissions cuts can be huge. For example, reducing emissions enough to limit warming to 2°C over the next century implies a global *net* cost of between $2.4 trillion and $26.5 trillion.[19] The example is not hypothetical. The EU has adopted the 2°C limit as its (declarative) climate policy.[20]

Second, hard caps also encourage premature emissions reductions. Greenhouse gases are a "stock" pollutant. The harm they may cause results from their concentration in the atmosphere. Because most greenhouse gases are long-lived, emissions can, over time, cause a gradual rise in atmospheric concentrations, but the rate of emission in any given year is comparatively unimportant. Thus, reducing *cumulative* emissions over decades is important; the rapidity with which they diminish is not.

Yet speed is expensive. Early emission cuts compel businesses to retire capital prematurely, an expensive proposition. Demanding that reductions occur quickly limits the potential for technological progress to lower abatement costs. Nevertheless, most environmental activists are aggressively pushing governments to implement needlessly hasty cuts that would entail high costs without any added benefit.

Third, hard caps lead to highly volatile allowance prices. In the American nitrous oxide (NO_x) program, allowance prices have fluctuated widely and rapidly. Recently, the price of allowances under the Clean Air Act's Title IV sulfur dioxide (SO_x) program has skyrocketed.[21]

The NO_x and SO_x emissions trading programs are small and simple compared to the complexities of trading GHG credits, since greenhouse gases are much more common and involve literally every sector of the economy. The business cycle, weather, economic growth, fuel prices, technological innovation, and changing social preferences will all cause fluctuations in the price of GHG allowances. The large number of for-profit firms seeking to manage these costs for fuel producers and consumers suggests the scale of the risk-management problem caused by hard caps.

With GHG emissions, price volatility would be far more economically significant than it has been with the NO_x and SO_x programs. With a GHG cap-and-trade system, emissions allowances become a necessary adjunct to fossil fuel consumption. The annual value of SO_x allowances has been around $2 billion, although it will rise with allowance prices. The annual initial value of a modest GHG cap-and-trade program could be $40 billion. GHG emissions allowances, therefore, would become an economically important commodity.

The current allowance price gyrations within the European Union's Emission Allowance Trading System (EU-ETS) are exactly what this history teaches one to expect. In the program's brief life, allowance prices skyrocketed, then plummeted, and now they are again rising. There is no knowing when the next lurch will occur:

> We have preliminary indications that European trading prices for CO_2 are highly volatile, fluctuating in a

band and +50 percent over the last year. More exten-
sive evidence comes from the history of the U.S. sulfur-
emissions trading program. SO_2 trading prices have
varied from a low of $70 per ton in 1996 to $1500 per
ton in late 2005. SO_2 allowances have a monthly volatility of 10 percent and an annual volatility of 43 percent
over the last decade.[22]

Businesses must find hedges against the unpredictability and
volatility of future allowance prices. In making investments, they
should take account of the social and environmental damage that
future GHG emissions will cause. Unlike allowance prices, though,
damage from GHG emissions does not gyrate unpredictably. The
costs of hedging against the allowance-price instability are a complete
waste, occasioned solely by the use of such quantitative caps as the
emissions control policy.

Cumulatively, these factors imply that, for any given level of emissions reduction, hard caps are likely to be very costly. In fact, compared to an emissions tax, quantitative limits will be up to five times
less cost-effective.[23] Because the Kyoto Protocol is based on hard
caps, it necessarily suffers from this low cost-effectiveness.

The Continuing Problem of Kyoto

The Clinton administration signed the Kyoto Protocol but had no
prospects of winning its ratification. By the end of the Clinton administration, therefore, national climate policy was at an impasse, unable
either to advance or retreat.

Upon taking office, the Bush administration swiftly extricated
the United States from this untenable position. The administration's
bold rejection of the protocol, however, set the country at odds with
its traditional western and central European allies. The brusque man-
ner in which the administration announced the decision further
bruised European feelings.

In dealing with Kyoto, the Bush administration has "scotch'd the
snake, not killed it." Despite America's rejection, the Kyoto Protocol

did not die; in fact, in 2005, it achieved the participation level needed for it to come into force. Its existence still plagues American—and international—climate policy.

The protocol creates hazards for foreign politicians seeking more promising solutions. Thus, British Prime Minister Tony Blair, once a strong supporter, expressed skepticism in 2005 about the prospects for negotiating another major climate-change mitigation treaty like Kyoto. He called for the exploration of other approaches.[24] British Greens subjected him to a torrent of vituperative criticism.[25] Ultimately, Blair was forced to recant publicly his flirtation with realism.[26]

Additionally, the Kyoto Protocol has become an evergreen rallying cry that anti-American politicians seek to exploit for partisan electoral advantage. At the Montreal climate summit, Paul Martin's strident criticism of the American position on Kyoto was aimed at voters in the impending Canadian elections at least as much as it was directed at influencing the negotiations. Similarly, during the German election of 2005, then–environment minister Jirgen Trittin claimed that Bush climate policy had caused the damage occasioned by Hurricane Katrina.[27] Trittin had clearly calculated that a public fight with America over Kyoto would mobilize green voters to support the anti-American Red-Green Coalition.

In the past, larger shared interests might have softened European criticism of American climate policy. But the end of the Soviet threat has eliminated Europe's strongest incentive for muting conflicts with the United States. At the same time, it has diminished the importance to the United States of the opinions of its traditional western and central European allies.[28] Nevertheless, Europe remains important, and concern about American diplomatic isolation has, in general, lent European criticism some domestic political traction.[29] Some of this sensitivity is probably transitory, a longing for a bygone era that will fade as Americans accustom themselves to the new constellation of national interests.

At Montreal, the parties to the Kyoto Protocol agreed to begin negotiations about a possible second commitment period beginning in 2012. This decision was predicated on speculation that the Bush administration's successor might be willing to return to the Kyoto negotiations. Former President Clinton appeared at this event. He urged the Europeans to continue trying to use state and local governments to subvert the American government's position.

On the one hand, this extraordinary performance is a reminder that the Kyoto Protocol, despite its substantive futility, may possess unexpected political vigor. As during the initial Kyoto negotiations, American Greens constitute a fifth column working to undermine the United States' resistance to the agreement. Any future president cultivating the environmental vote would feel some domestic political temptation to "lose" a climate negotiation with the Europeans. And countervailing industry opposition to GHG cap-and-trade has gradually weakened, as a growing number of businesses seek to position themselves to profit from a carbon-constrained economy.

On the other hand, Kyoto can be plausibly portrayed as an energy tax that transfers American money abroad. Much of the electorate, if informed, will resist it. American conservatives oppose, on principle, extension of government control over the economy. And the structure of the legislative process, especially in the Senate, facilitates defense of the status quo, especially when the White House is also opposed to new policies. At the least, the United States seems unlikely to approve another agreement as blatantly deleterious as the one signed by President Clinton.

American conservatives still cherish hopes of avoiding U.S. accretion to any version of Kyoto. They speculate that Kyoto's internal contradictions may cause it to collapse relatively soon. The Kyoto coalition is narrow. The GHG limits create competitive disadvantages for countries vis-à-vis their major trading partners.[30] The more visible the Kyoto-induced economic malaise becomes, the less inclined other countries will be to join it.

Nonetheless, many European countries are already institutionalizing Byzantine climate policy regimes. Germany, for instance, has an industrial GHG cap-and-trade system as well as an ecological (energy) tax. It has laws forcing utilities to buy renewable power at above market prices. It has astronomical fuel taxes and a diesel fuel tax differential. It has stringent building codes, quasi-mandatory corporate average fuel economy (CAFE) standards, and other expensive and intrusive regulations. Other European counties' climate policies mimic the German legal labyrinth.

Inevitably, a large organizational infrastructure is springing up around each of these institutions—regulatory bureaucracies, green parties, nongovernmental organizations (NGOs), subsidized businesses, renewable energy producers, firms that gain as regulations harm their competitors, and lawyers and consultants paid to navigate the baroque legal architecture.

Subsequent steps down the road to eco-serfdom may become ever easier. Organizations favored by the new law are likely to gain wealth and power relative to those that are disfavored. The latter interests, especially multinational corporations, may simply decamp to friendlier regulatory climes.

Ideology, too, can play a role in sustaining dysfunctional institutions. Historically, despite the manifestly poor performance of *dirigiste* economies, Marxist ideologies effectively rationalized and justified their failures.[31] Today, environmentalist ideology rationalizes and justifies economically harmful climate policies. For many Europeans, it apparently does so convincingly. If Kyoto's high costs and small benefits were enough to ensure Europe's rejection of it, the sclerotic, overregulated European "social-market" regimes would long since have vanished.

Finally, the Kyoto system's Clean Development Mechanism (CDM) encourages China and India to remain within Kyoto. Under CDM, Europe and Japan pay countries like China and India to initiate projects using particular technologies that are supposedly "climate-friendly." In exchange, the industrialized countries receive credits to apply against their Kyoto targets. Although these projects may enable China and India to avoid some potential emissions, they don't prevent those countries from increasing their emissions in other ways.

As climate policy, the system is fraught with problems. Arbitrary political decisions cramp its cost-effectiveness. For example, nuclear power projects cannot qualify under the CDM. The rules require that projects qualify only if they would not be built without the CDM. This requirement mires the entire process in counterfactual speculation. In itself, project-by-project decision-making entails high transaction costs.

Nonetheless, for China and India, the CDM is a source of additional development aid, albeit one with multiple strings attached. European countries (and their companies), desperate to meet Kyoto targets, are a potentially rich source of income. And the CDM helps to establish the principle that others must pay China and India to reduce GHG emissions. Hence, the CDM encourages China and India to shy away from any policy that would disrupt the good deal they have received under Kyoto, and the Kyoto industrialized countries can hope that a future liberalization of CDM rules will release a broad, swift river of less expensive emissions allowances that will help them reduce the cost of meeting their Kyoto targets. The CDM, as a result, has become an important prop of the Kyoto system.

Constructing an Alternative to the Kyoto Regime

Notwithstanding nearly unanimous political criticism, opposition to Kyoto has, properly, remained the polestar by which President Bush has steered his administration's international climate policy. But since the administration has promised to do nothing actively to disrupt the Kyoto process, American officials have refrained from explicit interference with the evolution of the protocol. The tone of their public comments is typically muffled. Yet the president himself continues to note the protocol's harmful potential impacts on the American economy.

The Bush administration's position at the 2005 Montreal Conference of the Parties (COP) to the United Nations Framework Convention on Climate Change (UNFCCC) illustrated its continuing strong resistance to Kyoto, as well as the difficulties in maintaining (and advancing) that position. At that meeting, the administration's foreign and domestic climate-policy foes sought to entangle it in negotiations about the protocol's post-2012 future. In doing so, they sought to bolster Kyoto's tottering credibility. American negotiators tenaciously resisted these machinations.

The U.S. delegation at Montreal also sought to avoid the seeming insensitivity of its earlier withdrawal from the protocol. In the end,

FIGURE 1

BUSH ADMINISTRATION INTERNATIONAL CLIMATE CHANGE INITIATIVES

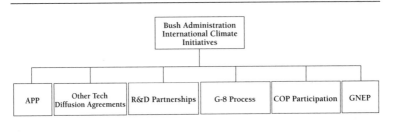

SOURCE: Author's illustration.

the administration gave nothing on substance. It agreed to participate in workshops about hypothetical future climate regimes. The Kyoto proponents trumpeted this "concession" as proof of the agreement's viability; administration representatives (slightly *sotto voce*) disputed this interpretation.

After rejecting the protocol, the United States government continued to recognize its UNFCCC obligations. It continued to participate in the COP talks and maintained observer status at the Kyoto talks. American policy rejects cap-and-trade programs for GHGs but seeks other means of reducing emissions while advancing climate-change science and technology. Doubtless hoping to dampen enthusiasm for Kyoto, the administration has fashioned an alternative international climate policy. It centers, instead, on technology diffusion and R&D. Figure 1 (above) illustrates the various initiatives.

By far the most important agreement is the Asia-Pacific Partnership for Clean Development and Climate (APP). The administration's representatives have worked diligently, and with some obvious initial success, to forge this agreement. The participants are Australia, China, India, Japan, South Korea, and the United States.

> The Partnership's vision statement . . . identifies a broad
> range of near- and long-term technologies and practices
> that are designed to improve energy security, reduce

pollution and address the long-term challenge of climate change. The Partnership focuses on voluntary practical measures to create new investment opportunities, build local capacity, and remove barriers to the introduction of cleaner, more efficient technologies. It is important to build on mutual interests and provide incentives to tackle shared global challenges such as climate change effectively.[32]

The administration's description of how the APP will achieve these goals states:

A principal, operational objective of the Partnership is to identify profitable technology investment opportunities and outcomes in each partner country. While there may be discussion of "demonstration projects" related to emerging technologies in each sector, we are placing a strong emphasis on identifying opportunities for near-term outcomes that can be "mass produced" using tried and true technologies and methods.[33]

The Environmental Protection Agency's so-called Methane to Markets initiative is the model for the APP.[34] The concept is that many opportunities exist for profitably reducing GHG emissions with existing technologies. Government, in cooperation with the private sector, will identify these opportunities. It will encourage projects to confirm the economic appeal of emissions-reduction technologies. It is hoped that the success of these projects will foster imitators and the adoption of new standard practices by business. President Bush's FY 2007 budget asks for $52 million to support the APP. It is not clear, however, whether good analogues to methane capture exist in other areas.

The new APP agreement establishes eight technology-centered working groups designed to create public-private partnerships:

- Cleaner Fossil Energy
- Renewable Energy and Distributed Generation

- Power Generation and Transmission
- Steel
- Aluminum
- Cement
- Coal Mining
- Buildings and Appliances

It is possible the APP could adopt as its strategic beacon efforts to identify and remove government-imposed economic distortions that discourage investment in more modern (and lower GHG-emitting) technologies. Some remarks by Energy Secretary Bodman sound this theme:

> As we heard yesterday at the Business Dialogue, the private sector is looking to us in government to provide a predictable environment in which investment and collaboration on clean energy technologies can occur. That includes respect for intellectual property rights, protection for the sanctity of contracts, and the establishment of a level playing field where laws and regulations are clear and consistently enforced. If we are not dependable, we can hardly expect the private sector to function with confidence . . . or effectiveness.[35]

In this vein, economist David Montgomery has argued that institutional reform in China and India could be a powerful tool for climate policy:

> Opportunities exist because the technology of energy use in developing countries embodies far higher emissions per dollar of output than does technology used in the United States; this is true of new investment in countries like China and India as well as their installed base . . . The technology embodied in the installed base of capital

equipment in China produces emissions at about 4 times the rate of technology in use in the United States. China's . . . new investment embodies technology with twice the emissions intensity of new investment in the United States. India is making almost no improvement in its emissions intensity. . . . India's new investment also embodies technology with twice the emissions intensity of new investment in the United States.[36]

Relatively efficient markets and strong legal institutions predominate in developed economies like the United States. Such economies, therefore, offer few opportunities for profitably enhancing energy efficiency. As efficiency-enhancing technologies arise, competitive markets spur their adoption.

No such assurance exists in China and India. Due to institutional and market failures, those countries' economic systems lack incentives for efficient energy use. Investment climates that discourage foreign investment and technology also afflict the Chinese and Indian economies. According to Montgomery, "Remedying these institutional and market failures offers the prospect of reconciling economic growth and emissions reduction."[37]

In China and India, several types of policy-induced economic distortions discourage adoption of more energy-efficient technologies. Examples include underpricing of electricity in India and coal transportation subsidies in China. Other policies discourage foreign direct investment that would be likely to help modernize the technological base, including the absence of the rule of law, weak protection of intellectual property, crypto-subsidies to state-owned enterprises, and inadequate access to foreign capital. Lack of infrastructure, education, and skills required for technology also contributes.[38]

Implicitly, Montgomery's analysis questions the significance of the APP. If he is correct, the environmental effectiveness of the APP hinges on its success in achieving institutional reform, rather than promoting specific technology demonstration projects (following the "Methane to Markets" model). Four points are pertinent:

First, if the APP does not focus on removing policy-induced distortions, it will be ineffectual. "A hostile economic environment in China and India will prevent technology that is introduced through projects that the Partnership might support from spreading throughout the economy," says Montgomery.[39] In that case, a technically successful demonstration project will accomplish little. Obviously, if the APP produces only isolated demonstration projects, it will not significantly reduce GHG emissions, although it will not cost much either. The rise in world energy prices has made many off-the-shelf technologies newly profitable. The diffusion of these technologies might confer a public relations windfall on the APP, but this trend will not indicate the partnership's effectiveness as climate policy.

Second, where no institutional barrier blocks the adoption of a new technology, the demonstration of its virtues may be a good thing, but its value is necessarily relatively limited. Unless a market failure impedes their adoption, market forces will soon prompt the introduction of cost-effective, energy-saving innovations. Demonstration projects might slightly accelerate the harvest, which would be a good thing, but eventually the market will have reaped the gains in any case.

Third, even the optimal APP strategy of attacking market distortions will yield gains small in comparison to the scale of anthropogenic climate change. By 2017, the maximum impact from Chinese and Indian adoption of U.S. technology will eliminate 7,700 million metric tons of cumulative carbon emissions. This will be a significant achievement in the Kyoto context; by that time, the protocol aspires to reduce emissions by about the same amount—7,300 million metric tons. And, unlike the Kyoto Protocol, economic reform in China and India will produce net benefits, so a reform-oriented APP, if it works, will be a superior policy. Even so, the potential environmental benefits are modest: The Bush administration has repeatedly observed that the protocol's goals, even if achieved, will do little to slow the pace of warming. The administration cannot logically castigate Kyoto's environmental benefits as paltry while touting those of APP as environmentally significant.

Fourth, the institutional change needed to produce even these results will be hard to achieve. Certainly, both China and India have shown that they can make some institutional change in the interest of faster economic development. But such change remains limited. Strong interests will resist reforms of the kind needed to reduce energy consumption rapidly. The richer APP countries have a limited ability to dislodge the relevant special interests from their positions of power. These considerations suggest that the economic reform strategy may produce far smaller GHG reductions than are theoretically possible.

Whether the APP represents an effective political counter to the Kyoto Protocol also remains to be seen. Australia and the United States are industrialized countries that have rejected Kyoto. China and India are Kyoto participants but have declined to accept limits. Japan is the largest economy that has assumed a Kyoto target. (Parts of the Japanese government are clearly concerned about the competitiveness implications of the protocol.)

The American government, understandably, disputes claims that the APP is aimed at countering Kyoto. Under Secretary of State Paula Dobriansky has remarked, "We do not see this [APP] as a replacement. We see it as a complement to the Kyoto Protocol."[40] In the short run, that statement is true. It is politically correct and diplomatic. The administration is prudent to make this assertion.

Nonetheless, the principles behind the APP are very different from Kyoto's. And no international climate protection regime can be viable without China, India, Japan, and the United States. All these countries have motives for seeking an alternative to the protocol. If Kyoto loses political momentum, the APP offers a golden bridge over which Japan and Canada (which is not yet part of the APP) can retreat to a less confrontational form of climate policy. Building such a bridge is in America's national inter-est, but proclaiming that purpose explicitly is politically counterproductive at this point.

Beyond the APP, the recent Energy Policy Act directs the Department of State to encourage diffusion of climate-friendly technologies. The amendment appears to target market distortions in the major developing-world emitters. Largely crafted by Senator Hagel, the legislation mandates an inventory of such technologies. It directs (in Title XVI) the State Department and the U.S. Trade Representative to identify and seek ways to surmount barriers to the diffusion of the technologies.

So far, the Bush administration, although it supported enactment of Title XVI, has not done the analyses needed to implement it. The Department of Energy argues that Congress failed to provide funding for these requirements—but DOE failed to reprogram money from other areas, although the sums involved are trivial in comparison with the department's overall budget or even its administrative accounts. That decision suggests a weak commitment to this initiative (and perhaps management difficulties). In principle, though, the work now starting under the aegis of the APP could contribute to implementing Title XVI.

The APP and Title XVI both concentrate on technology diffusion. The same description fits EPA's "Methane to Markets" program. The administration has negotiated twenty or so lesser international agreements on climate-related technology diffusion.

The Bush administration has also constructed a series of international climate-related R&D agreements. These agreements are designed to foster cooperation on technology development, technology transfer, and climate science. The various R&D agreements are coalitions of the willing, constructed outside of the UNFCCC process. Most are organized around specific technologies. They cover nuclear power, hydrogen as an energy carrier, coal gasification, and carbon sequestration. Another agreement advances "earth observation" technologies. As Under Secretary Dobrianski has observed,

> We . . . value the multilateral initiatives we have launched: the Generation IV Nuclear Initiative; the Global Earth Observation Initiative; the Carbon Sequestration Leadership Forum; the International Partnership for the Hydrogen Economy; and the Clean Energy Initiative.[41]

For the most part, these agreements seem directed toward technological information-sharing, although the hydrogen energy negotiations have begun to address issues of international technology standards.

The existing R&D agreements are not particularly ambitious. For example, although the United States has concluded international information-sharing agreements on several climate-related technologies, most do not yet entail formal R&D cost-sharing. R&D exhibits some of the global public good features that plague the larger climate-change issue. Hence, there is need for cooperative solutions.[42]

With R&D, in contrast to emissions controls, the resulting free-rider problem may be more tractable. Successful climate-related R&D may confer large economic rewards on innovators. And R&D is likely to be inexpensive compared with the imposition of stringent GHG controls. Still, cooperation would decrease free riding. By doing so, it would move the level of effort closer to optimum.[43]

Another relevant American R&D program is on an uncharacteristically fast track. With the Global Nuclear Energy Partnership (GNEP), the Bush administration reversed previous American opposition to nuclear fuel recycling. GNEP, which proposes a new model for the international management of the nuclear fuel cycle, has major R&D elements as well. GNEP involves projects to demonstrate innovative nuclear fuel recycling technologies. Other projects seek to demonstrate technology that could eventually lead to economically viable breeder reactors.

Large-scale deployment of new nuclear power plants potentially offers important advantages for climate policy. However, uranium supply has limited the creation of new plants. While adequate for current capacity, the supply cannot accommodate a very large expansion. Spent fuel disposal is another major constraint.

Hypothetically, fuel recycling and nuclear breeder reactors could solve these problems. But worries about proliferation and terrorism impede fuel recycling. GNEP's proposed international fuel cycle agreement attacks these security concerns. Its technology demonstrations, if successful, could boost fuel supply while simultaneously diminishing spent-fuel disposal problems, making nuclear power a more attractive climate policy solution. Hence, GNEP's success would spell a major climate policy advance. Critics rightly point to technical difficulties and serious economic challenges.[44] But this program does appear to be a high priority for the administration, and it is operating on an aggressive schedule, bolstered by presidential support.

GNEP's relatively high priority suggests that the Bush administration largely follows a "no regrets" policy on climate-related technologies.[45] While it happily claims credit for programs that promise climate policy benefits, its resource commitments are heavily influenced by nonclimate concerns. With GNEP, climate considerations reinforce higher-priority antiproliferation and energy supply motivations. (GNEP is seeking a technological solution to the proliferation concerns that have heretofore impeded reliance on fuel recycling.) Nevertheless, GNEP's success would confer significant climate policy gains. This pattern is not necessarily bad. It raises the question of whether a policy confined to a no-regrets basis can provide a strong enough response to a problem of the potential magnitude of climate change.

In addition to launching its own climate technology initiatives, the Bush administration has reacted to others'. In 2005, British Prime Minister Tony Blair was chairman of the G8. He used that position to entangle the Bush administration in a G8 negotiation on climate policy. The Bush administration would have preferred not to handle this matter at the G8.

Notwithstanding these reservations, the United States emerged rather well from the negotiation's first round. The Gleneagles G8 summit communiqué reflected the administration's emphasis on technology and on multiple approaches to climate policy. In theory, subsequent meetings will revisit this theme. But the G8's rotating presidency hinders continuity. In retrospect, the Gleneagles summit's focus on climate may have been a one-time event.

Conclusion

The Bush administration had strong reasons for rejecting the Kyoto Protocol. America's rejection did not, however, kill Kyoto. The agreement poses a series of challenges to the U.S. government. At this point, its long-term durability is unforeseeable.

In response to this continuing threat, the administration has constructed an alternative climate policy that rejects economy-wide mandatory GHG emissions and features technology transfer and R&D.

The APP is the most visible component of the American alternative to Kyoto. Its effectiveness is likely to depend heavily on the degree to which it produces institutional changes in China and India. Another approach, GNEP, might unlock a longer-term option of greatly expanding the scope of nuclear power. GNEP, however, faces formidable technical and economic difficulties. So far the administration has not proposed the "obvious" international agreement of reciprocal increases in funding of climate-related R&D.

The administration has diligently pursued its initiatives. Nonetheless, on its face, the current policy cannot make a large impact on the rate of climate change. Partly for that reason, it has not eliminated the threat posed by the Kyoto Protocol.

2

The Chimera of Global GHG Cap-and-Trade

Some critics reproach President Bush for failing to propose an alternative mandatory emissions control scheme. The Bush administration's error, in this view, was in not presenting an alternative architecture. To the critics, some version of international cap-and-trade can be salvaged and represents the best possible way forward. The arguments for this proposition are weak.

There are several reasons to doubt the basic realism of international GHG controls:

- Kyoto's environmental ineffectuality seems incurable. Aggressive GHG abatement will incur net costs, not net benefits. Within Kyoto's existing structure, ratcheting up the agreement's stringency would escalate costs much faster than benefits. Such an agreement is clearly unacceptable to most of the world.

- GHG controls are very unlikely to stimulate the kind and scale of technological innovation required to reduce abatement costs dramatically. The needed innovations require basic science and very long-run R&D. The private sector, even if subjected to GHG limits, does not have sufficient incentives to produce such innovation.

- Although scientific discoveries may increase the perceived threat of climate change, this effect may be offset by more realistic modeling of abatement costs. Institutional factors are likely to cause real-world abatement to be far more expensive than economic models estimate. In the event, both damage estimates and expected abatement costs may rise, leaving estimated net benefits unchanged.

- Ultimately, proponents of international GHG controls count on being able somehow to buy cheap emission cuts from China and India, but institutional difficulties may preclude this option. In any case, the absence of efficient markets and the rule of law will cause Chinese and Indian emissions reductions to be considerably more expensive than is typically assumed.

- Although proponents cite the Montreal Protocol and the agreements creating the WTO as proof that international GHG limits can be made to work, these analogies are false and misleading. Unlike the WTO and the Montreal Protocol, aggressive GHG controls are likely to entail net costs for most participants. Other factors make the WTO and Montreal analogies even more misleading.

Proposals to Ratchet Up Kyoto's Stringency

Kyoto's apologists know that the agreement offers anemic benefits. They remain untroubled. The Kyoto Protocol, they correctly remind us, was intended merely as a stepping stone. Eventually, in this view, successor agreements will force transformation of the entire global energy system, which is required to halt anthropogenic climate change. The reality is otherwise.

First, Kyoto's structure is so defective that it cannot be scaled up to achieve substantial results—an inconvenient truth indeed. Simple arithmetic can illustrate Kyoto's incorrigible cost-effectiveness deficiency. As already mentioned, one estimate is that the pre-Marrakech version of Kyoto would have reduced global mean temperatures by .03°C. To truly blunt the threat of climate change, a policy would need to have roughly one hundred times that impact. (A 3°C decrease in global mean temperature is required to bring the high-end estimates of this century's possible temperature increases into the range generally conceded to be "safe.") As mentioned above, the mean estimate from the various economic models of Kyoto's impact on the U.S. GDP is –.59 percent. If abatement costs increase only linearly with stringency, a hypothetical maxi-Kyoto will cut U.S. GDP by 59 percent.

Second, *ceteris paribus*, as GHG controls increase in stringency, abatement costs will rise faster than do benefits. Hence, only mild and gradual GHG controls seem likely to yield net benefits.[1] The main difficulty is technology. Large GHG reductions will entail drastically reducing fossil fuel consumption. With current technology, sharply restricting fossil fuel consumption will reduce capital and labor productivity.

True, gentle control policies seemingly yield net benefits. The reverse of that coin is that they slow climate change only very slightly. The Nordhaus-Boyer results, for example, suggest that even by the end of this century, an economically efficient policy will reduce total emissions by only 11 percent below baseline.[2] Controls will be so superficial that annual emissions will nearly double during the course of the current century.[3] Obviously, atmospheric GHG concentrations will continue rising.

Consequently, although this unambitious policy appears to yield net benefits, those benefits are small. The present value of the global projected net benefit from one version of optimal policy is only $200 billion.[4] Will such small benefits justify the nontrivial transaction costs of maintaining a global GHG control regime for more than a century? It is quite possible that they will not. In any case, such soft controls are hardly what Kyoto's proponents have in mind.

Assessing the Rationale for International Cap-and-Trade

Advocates for international cap-and-trade dispute these doubts; they contend that ambitious GHG control regimes are both possible and desirable. Economic models, they assert, overstate abatement costs. The models miss the policy-induced technological changes that cap-and-trade would call forth. Moreover, new scientific discoveries might raise estimates for damage expected from climate change. In this view, nations will do what is necessary to abate GHG emissions. Unfortunately, neither of these assertions withstands careful scrutiny.

Consider first the claim that GHG cap-and-trade will induce a torrent of private sector R&D. To some degree, placing a price on carbon emissions must occasion some change in the pattern of private sector R&D. Although most economic models assume some constant rate of technological advance, they do not consider this policy-induced acceleration of innovation. The omission may, indeed, lead to some overstatement of future abatement costs. But how big is the overstatement? And do the models also contain other offsetting biases?

In fact, the induced-innovation effect of GHG limits will be small, and the models, by using overly optimistic assumptions about the efficiency of abatement policies, probably contain much larger optimistic biases about future abatement costs. Consider first the likely size of technological innovation induced by GHG controls.

All economists recognize that market forces call forth a less than optimal quantity of R&D. Once a private sector innovator demonstrates the feasibility and profitability of a new technology, competitors are likely to imitate it, thus escaping the high fixed costs required to make the original discovery. Copycats, therefore, can gain market share by undercutting the innovator's prices. By doing so, they deprive the initial developer of most of his hypothetical financial gain. Foreseeing this competitive contretemps, firms avoid investment in many R&D projects that might otherwise be profitable.[5]

The private sector's reluctance to rely on R&D strategies is likely to be especially strong with the kind of activities needed to reduce GHG emissions. Since no large emissions-free energy sources lie just over the horizon,[6] successful innovation in this area will require unusually high risks and long delays; and because developing these technologies will entail breakthroughs in basic science, much of the most essential work will be ineligible for patent protection. These are precisely the conditions in which firms are least likely to rely on R&D as an approach to problem-solving.[7]

It follows, then, that the principal strategies for coping with greenhouse gas controls are likely to consist of substitution among existing technologies, not R&D.[8] GHG controls would eliminate firms' tendencies to treat atmospheric disposal of GHGs as a free service—but they will not eliminate the market disincentives for using R&D as a response to controls. Thus, GHG limits will only modestly increase private sector R&D directed toward technological solutions to GHG abatement.[9]

In any case, policies proposing future emissions controls suffer from a credibility problem. Given the private sector's incentives to underinvest in R&D, only the prospect of very high future emissions costs would induce firms to make large R&D investments. Yet investors must question whether future governments would actually implement draconian emissions cuts. Today's officeholders flinch from doing so; why should future politicians be more reckless in imposing costs on constituents and campaign contributors? By inference, any future GHG control costs low enough to be politically credible will be too low to stimulate the needed level of R&D. And any costs high enough to stimulate R&D will not be credible.[10]

Policy-induced technological innovation, then, does not convincingly promise to lower GHG abatement costs dramatically. The most realistic prediction is that abatement will remain expensive and, consequently, most governments will decline to buy much of it. Accounting for the induced-innovation effect, then, is unlikely to fortify greatly the rationale for international GHG controls or to enhance their prospects for success.

The possibility that climate change may be more harmful than initially believed is probably a more powerful argument. New climate-science discoveries emerge constantly. Some are disturbing. Also, current climate-change damage estimates omit many factors that could be important.[11] *Ceteris paribus*, more comprehensive damage estimates should raise nations' willingness to pay for abatement—even if abatement costs remain high. Even so, other factors may offset alarming new science.

One such countervailing factor is that *definitive* scientific evidence has been hard to find. Estimates of climate sensitivity—the amount of warming expected to result from a doubling of atmospheric carbon dioxide concentrations—continue to differ widely. According to a

recent MIT model, "Absent mitigation policies, the median projection
. . . shows a global average temperature rise from 1990 to 2100 of
2.4°C, with a 95 percent confidence interval of 1.0°C to 4.9°C . . ."[12]

Nonscientific factors also magnify the uncertainties about the
extent of future climate change:

> Development of such projections is a complex task
> because the analysis must consider uncertainties not
> only in the climate system response, but also in popula-
> tion growth, economic development and technological
> change, and it must take into account potential feed-
> backs among these systems over time should climate
> change occur.[13]

In estimating the economic significance of climate change, human
adaptation compounds the difficulty of the analysis.[14]

The main economic rationale for abatement actually rests on the
low-likelihood but high-damage potential upper end of the probability distribution of temperature estimates. Logically, today's continuing
uncertainties about climate sensitivity should reinforce a willingness
to invest in mitigation. Yet popular political psychology may interpret
the large uncertainties as diminishing the need for action. (It sometimes appears that President Bush's science advisors have failed fully
to disabuse him of this fallacy.)

Moreover, while climate-change damage estimates may rise, other
aspects of the climate policy landscape are also changing. Most
importantly, recent political events (like the policies that are actually
being implemented in Europe and proposed in the United States)
indicate that the GHG abatement cost estimates of the various models are biased downward. If so, better economic analysis may increase
abatement cost estimates just as new science is increasing the estimated abatement benefits. The net effect could be modest, and its
direction is uncertain.

The root of the difficulty with abatement cost estimates is that
the relevant economic models predicate them on use of idealized,
frictionless carbon taxes, or on even more highly idealized versions

of cap-and-trade. As already discussed, actual policies are sector-specific and based on hard caps, and they contain large elements of command-and-control regulation. All three features severely degrade the cost-effectiveness of controls. Constructing an international GHG control regime, moreover, is not free. These costs, though ignored by the economic models, will affect the way governments view such a project.

The remainder of this chapter will suggest that the effects of the economists' earlier simplifying assumptions about abatement costs are likely to be large. It will also argue that the factors that degrade the cost-effectiveness of GHG control regimes are systematic and anchored in the very nature of democratic institutions. As such, even the most vigorous proselytizing by well-intentioned economists is likely to fall on deaf ears—as it has to date.

The High Costs of National and International GHG Control Regimes

As illustrated by EU policies and current American GHG control proposals, governments impose very inefficient GHG control measures in practice. Most such measures are sector-specific; many employ command-and-control mechanisms. Some are inefficiently structured cap-and-trade plans; others are subsidies or government-mandated cross-subsidies. The control levels are set arbitrarily. Policies overlap and conflict.

Virtually all economists would agree that the real-world policy packages are needlessly costly. The policies are not, however, merely the product of policymakers' confusion and ignorance (which is not to deny that some policymakers are confused and ignorant). Rather, deeply rooted features of the political economies of modern democracies engender inefficient policies.

One such feature is the wide variation in the ability of social sectors to affect government policy. All sectors seek to evade paying the costs of GHG controls. As political systems respond differentially to the more influential sectors' demands, a patchwork of controls and cost-shifting policies emerges. Economists tirelessly preach the virtues of economy-wide controls and uniform marginal abatement costs across sectors; political systems almost unanimously ignore their sermons. The logic of economic efficiency clashes with the logic of political bargaining. And the latter wins because it better serves the decision-makers' own needs.

A second apposite feature of political economy is that implementing climate policy requires assembling an intragovernmental winning coalition. Most policy processes are somewhat balkanized; multiple semi-independent centers compete for power, influence, and economic rents. The climate-change issue offers political actors variegated opportunities for institutional and individual self-aggrandizement. Bureaucracies, legislative committees, levels of government, and individual policy entrepreneurs all compete for a "piece of the action." A patchwork solution offers better opportunities for constructing a winning coalition than a unitary one.

A third feature is that governments seek to hide the costs of their policies while highlighting the benefits. Efforts to manipulate the "political optics" often increase the policies' total costs. Thus, many elected officials prefer command-and-control measures because the costs are less transparent than the more efficient emissions taxes.[15] Subsidies financed by either general revenue or borrowing have the same effect. The reelection incentive virtually guarantees the political appeal of these inefficient expedients.

Obviously, these three mechanisms interact and reinforce each other. The result is climate policy "like to a chaos" that carries no resemblance to the economists' visions of mild, uniform carbon taxes. In principle, strong and enlightened leadership could at least partially counteract the baleful incentives at large within the political process. The next chapter will consider why such climate policy leadership has so far failed to appear; the final chapter will ask if such leadership might be an option for the Bush administration. The remainder of this chapter will explain in greater depth reasons for skepticism about the prospects for effective international GHG controls.

While this discussion has so far concentrated on factors operating within national political systems, climate policies must function internationally. The transactions required to forge and maintain an international control regime add another layer of costs. In the American economy, for instance, more than 45 percent of national income is devoted to transacting.[16] Most economic models simply assume away these costs—a tremendously misleading practice.

The distortion becomes more acute in the case of building and maintaining an international GHG agreement, which would inevitably be transaction-intensive. Participants would have to negotiate and renegotiate terms. Lacking a third-party enforcer, the states most interested in creating an effective regime must bear the costs of enforcing the participation and compliance of less zealous nations. But these enforcement costs diminish and perhaps vitiate the expected net benefits that motivate the potential enforcers.[17]

The pervasive temptation of "free riding" would amplify the transaction costs. Free riding occurs because a nation, in determining how much to spend on abatement, considers only its own share of the benefits from reduced emissions. But even a large and vulnerable country would realize only a small share of the benefits derived from any abatement action it might undertake.

Thus, unless nations make and keep a cooperative agreement, they will dramatically underinvest in emissions controls. One study estimates that without cooperation, the level of abatement effort (as measured by marginal abatement costs) would, on average, be only $1/25th$ of what it would be with a fully cooperative outcome.[18] Indeed, without effective international cooperation, it would be economically rational for most countries to abstain entirely from controlling GHG emissions.[19]

Experience is confirming this analysis. For international GHG controls, free riding is pervasive. In fact, one or another form of it is far more common than abatement. Indeed, it is more common than even the *pretense* of abatement. The hole is much larger than the doughnut.

Free riding, even at levels far below that now prevalent with Kyoto, could fatally weaken international GHG controls. Countries operating without GHG controls encourage energy-intensive businesses and activities to migrate to their shores. In that case, nations with controls incur economic losses; yet they succeed only in changing the geographic pattern of emissions—not in reducing them. The entire control regime may unravel. Or it may never arise.

Under some conditions, international cooperation can overcome the tendency of countries to free-ride. By agreeing to curtail emissions if other nations do likewise, governments can leverage their own abatement policies. Such agreements could diminish the tendency to underabate.

Despite the potential advantages of cooperation, it often fails to emerge. History is full of examples. Many desirable international environmental agreements have collapsed. Some have never materialized. Others have merely ratified the status quo that would have prevailed given domestic political realities.[20] This historical record should remind us that international cooperation can be elusive, expensive, and sometimes mostly illusory.

Every step of the process of constructing an international GHG control regime is likely to be costly. The international negotiations needed to produce agreement on a greenhouse gas cap-and-trade program like Kyoto are extraordinarily complex. Furthermore, to keep the system in tune with the ever-changing economic, scientific, and political environment, negotiations must be continuous, not a one-time agreement:

> Any stringent regime would involve allocating emission rights worth trillions of dollars among rich nations and poor, rapidly growing nations and more mature economies, and countries with fossil fuels and countries without. I see no possibility of any such compact being arrived at. If there were such quotas, they would certainly have to be renegotiated periodically as estimates changed and as nations experienced greater and lesser difficulties. Any nation that "sold" part of its quota would clearly be evidencing a too generous original quota.[21]

Not all the costs will be in cash. The EU, for example, bought the legal fiction of Russian ratification of the Kyoto Protocol (which was necessary for the protocol to become legally binding) with concessions on the Russian bid for WTO membership. Presumably, these concessions entailed economic costs to the EU member states. If nothing else, the EU sacrificed the opportunity to use them as bargaining chips to gain Russian concessions in other negotiations.

Negotiations, though, are only one category of transaction costs. A successful international GHG pact would require that nations verify each other's compliance—a difficult task, and particularly problematic with a quantity-based emissions trading system like the Kyoto Protocol.

Governments vary greatly in honesty, transparency, and administrative effectiveness. By creating valuable emissions permits and allocating them to different countries, a cap-and-trade system in essence grants permit-holders the equivalent of authority to print money. The value of these permits can easily be used by a country's leaders for nonenvironmental purposes:[22]

> It would probably become common practice for dictators and corrupt administrators to sell part of their permits, pocket the proceeds, and enjoy wine, partners, and song along the Riviera. . . . Simulations suggest that tens of billions of dollars of permits may be available for export from Russia under the Kyoto Protocol. A Russian scientist recently reported that people in Moscow were already considering how to profit from the "privatization" of the Russian carbon emissions permits. Alternatively, consider the case of Nigeria, which had emissions of around 90 million tons of CO_2 emissions in recent years. If Nigeria could sell its allowances for $20 per ton under a "clean development mechanism" [CDM], this would raise around $2 billion each year of hard currency. This is in a country whose non-oil exports in 2000 were around $600 million.[23]

The need for aggressive monitoring is the inescapable corollary to this risk of abuse—a problem whose seriousness was confirmed by the recent United Nations "oil for food" scandal.[24] Conversely, the

CDM example suggests that stringent quality controls also imply high transaction costs.

Ultimately, international GHG controls must also incorporate *credible* enforcement mechanisms:

> Sanctions large enough to be effective deserve skepticism. Punishing poor countries will not be attractive; punishing rich countries, or large countries, or powerful countries, will not be attractive. I can imagine the United States agreeing to quotas it believes it can live with and making serious efforts to live within the quotas; it is hard to imagine any international body or consortium of nations imposing sanctions on the United States, or the United States accepting severe sanctions.[25]

Recent history bears out this skepticism about the political realism of sanctions. It suggests that, even in cases less difficult than climate change, sanctions are just not applied:

> Granting, for argument, the apparent logic that nations will not make sacrifices in the absence of sanctions, there is no historical example of any international regime that could impose penalties on a scale commensurate with the magnitude of global warming. (It is notable that the current most legally cohesive regime, the European Union—certainly stronger than any greenhouse regime that one could imagine—calls for severe penalties on any nation that runs a deficit greater than three percent of gross domestic product for three years running; in 2004 both France and Germany violated the rule, and nothing was expected to happen to those two nations, and nothing did happen.)[26]

The comparison may be extended beyond the issue of the relative strength of EU institutions and those of a future climate policy regime. It is also true that the causal connection between German and

French economic behavior and the continent's economic health is clearer and more immediate than that between any one nation's current emissions and global economic harm from climate change. If the Economic Stabilization Pact does not produce enforcement, why should one believe that a future agreement on climate change would do so?

The constellation of interests operating in the case of international GHG limits seems particularly inauspicious for the prospects of international cooperation. For instance, cooperation is more likely to emerge if solutions offer large net benefits. For the reasons discussed above, GHG limits do not appear to fit this case.[27] And alarming scientific discoveries may not reverse this judgment.

Then, too, not all countries gain from paying the marginal abatement costs needed to maximize global welfare; writes Robert Stavins, "For some countries, costs of control may exceed benefits."[28] These nations will probably reject simple agreements based on equal reciprocal abatement.

The fact that China and India fall into this category greatly exacerbates the problem. If one includes annual GHG emissions caused by changes in land use, those of less developed countries (LDCs) already exceed those of industrialized countries.[29] China and India are dominant sources of LDC emissions which are, moreover, growing more rapidly than those of other LDCs or of the OECD countries.

Indeed, it is impossible to stabilize atmospheric greenhouse gas concentrations at acceptable levels without constraining LDC emissions.[30] The greatest opportunities to reduce the growth in greenhouse gas emissions at relatively low cost are concentrated in China and India. Without the participation of these and similar countries, the largest reservoir of potentially affordable GHG abatement opportunities stands beyond reach. Moreover, if China and India decline to implement controls, stringent GHG limits in OECD countries would produce emissions leakage.[31]

Chinese and Indian participation is, therefore, a *sine qua non* of successful international GHG controls. Yet neither country is willing to pay significant costs to abate GHG emissions, and that fact is unlikely to change soon.

The Chinese and Indian governments' rejection of controls is rational. Giving priority to development makes sense, even from the standpoint of climate policy. Economic development enhances the capacity to adapt to climate change. It reduces dependence on the vulnerable agricultural and forestry sectors. It enhances the resource base available to respond to public health or infrastructure problems exacerbated by climate change. For China and India, adaptation is probably a better climate policy option than mitigation.[32] In any case, without development, LDCs cannot afford mitigation unless it is fully subsidized by wealthier countries.

Political factors reinforce the economic imperatives. Political legitimacy for both the Chinese and the Indian governmental systems depends heavily on the promise of rapid economic development. Both countries' histories exhibit powerful centrifugal tendencies and significant social unrest. Neither regime is under domestic pressure to diminish GHG emissions.

With China and India unwilling to institute controls, American options are severely constricted. Proponents of America's reentry into Kyoto (or of unilateral GHG limits) argue that these steps would transform Chinese and Indian incentives. A future American policy reversal would, they say, create an effective international regime. Once the United States joins this hypothetical control regime, the argument goes, China and India will follow suit.

This reasoning is mistaken. American GHG limits are a *necessary* condition for China and India to adopt controls—but they would not be a *sufficient* condition. American adoption of GHG limits would not weaken the disincentives that now deter the Chinese and Indian governments from promulgating GHG limits. True, China and India would gain competitively from unilateral imposition of American GHG controls. But the economies of these countries are more carbon-intensive than America's. Reciprocating America's move to controls would negate their gain and leave them worse off than they currently are vis-à-vis America. Additionally, adopting GHG limits would hobble India and China relative to other LDCs. And unless America's GHG controls were conditioned upon Chinese and Indian policies, those countries would have no incentive to change course.

Unilateral American controls cannot induce China and India to adopt controls. Making American controls contingent on Chinese and Indian reciprocation would be slightly less illogical, but, even so, that strategy is not likely to succeed. American emissions limits can only have a trivial impact on climate change, and China and India would reap little of those small benefits. As a bargaining chip, American controls are nearly worthless.

Experience confirms logic; the strategy has already been tried. After the United States signed the Kyoto Protocol, it was clear that the Senate would not ratify the agreement unless China and India accepted limits, so the Clinton administration sought reciprocal commitments from them. China was the key:

> On the president's 1998 trip to China, [White House Council of Economic Advisors (CEA) chairman] Yellen held several meetings with senior Chinese officials to discuss climate change policy, including the potential for indexed targets. Administration officials pressed the case in subsequent staff and political-level meetings with their Chinese counterparts. In 1999, CEA drafted an analysis of the potential gains from emissions trading for China and details about constructing an indexed emissions target. The administration transmitted this report to the Chinese government at the highest level. Despite these efforts, China repeatedly refused to adopt emissions commitments and erected barriers where possible to slow U.S. efforts to enlist other developing countries.[33]

This *demarche* failed, and nothing has happened since to change the actors' basic interests. The implications are stark. From a realistic climate policy perspective, the American demand for Chinese and Indian participation in emissions limitations is warranted. Yet China and India are rational to reject GHG cuts in favor of more urgent economic development priorities. If America is right to insist on reciprocation, and the Asian powers are rational to decline, there is no basis for agreement.

Some analysts hope that OECD countries, particularly America, will pay China and India to adopt GHG controls: "For a voluntary international mechanism to be successful, it must include a mechanism for transferring gains to countries that would otherwise not benefit from joining an agreement."[34] Thus, as Stavins has observed with regard to GHG controls, the LDCs must board the train; they do not have to pay for their own tickets.

Many proponents of this thinking see the United States adopting stringent GHG limits and then seeking to lower abatement costs by purchasing "cheap" abatement opportunities from China and India. In fact, this option is largely impracticable. Insightful economists have long cautioned that "side payments" would be harder to use in practice than theory might suggest.[35] In this case, practical problems abound.

To begin with, the scheme's feasibility depends on the United States's enacting stringent domestic controls. That prospect seems remote. Some domestic controls are likely, but ones stringent enough to generate the revenue needed to transform the Chinese and Indian economies are a fantasy.

Moreover, even if the United States were willing to pay abatement costs in China and India at all, it would do so only temporarily. Before agreeing to subsidize Chinese and Indian abatement, America would insist on agreement about when the subsidies would halt and how long abatement would continue. This would simply be another version of the current China/India problem. Compared with past efforts to construct such a bargain, it would be more favorable to China and India—and correspondingly less advantageous to the United States.

Still more fundamentally, institutional problems drastically narrow the prospects for realizing the large, cheap GHG cuts allegedly available in China and India. In fact, this supposed cornucopia of cheap abatement opportunities may not exist, or its bounty may be much exaggerated. There are two grounds for skepticism.

First, at the most obvious level, the possibility of international transfer payments creates powerful perverse incentives among prospective recipients and donors alike. If zealous states will pay reluctant states to abate, all governments have reason to feign indifference to climate change. They will also exaggerate their countries' expected emissions growth. (No antitrust laws can bar LDCs from conspiring to limit abatement offers in order to keep allowance prices high.)

Once the option of side-payments is in play, only countries with strong environmental movements will display concern with the problem. Domestic politics will trap these countries into donor status. As donor countries, they will have strong incentives to pretend to believe potential donees' inflated projections of emissions growth and exaggerated claims of abatement; doing so depresses global emissions allowance prices and avoids costly domestic abatement measures. The problem is manifest in the Clean Development Mechanism:

> Host countries gain from pretending not to care at all about energy efficiency. As a consequence, the net effect of actually reducing global CO_2 emissions will be small compared with the reported reduction. The likelihood of misrepresenting the true willingness to invest in energy efficiency by developing countries is increased by the fact that the industrialized country benefits from this cheating too. As a consequence, this proposal will presumably trigger little actual factual reduction in global CO_2 emissions.[36]

Other studies have reached very similar conclusions.[37]

Second, the earlier discussion of the Asia-Pacific Partnership adumbrated another equally refractory problem: When Chinese and Indian institutional realities are considered, these nations' abatement costs may be much higher than is commonly assumed. Because Chinese and Indian institutional barriers impede the use of efficient imported technology, actual technical costs of abatement may substantially exceed engineering estimates.

Moreover, the putative efficiency of market-based emissions controls depends on the premise of efficient markets operating under the impartially administered rule of law. Neither the Chinese nor the Indian energy sector exhibits these features. For example, in China, state-owned enterprises (SOEs), which are often owned by provinces or municipalities, have near-total control of the energy sector:

> Oil production and distribution has been concentrated in three large national SOEs, mostly non-competing. Electricity production is typically provided by provincial or municipal enterprises. China is having difficulty placing SOEs under tight budget constraints; they have historically had ready access to bank credit, and while banks (all themselves SOEs) are under instruction to make loans only on a commercial basis, local politics continues to play an important role in credit allocation, especially (I suspect) to energy firms.[38]

Such firms are unlikely to respond in textbook fashion to a carbon tax or emissions trading scheme. Indeed, with local governments as both owners and regulators of SOEs, corruption may be a more common response than textbook cost minimization. The Chinese judiciary is openly subservient to political institutions and the Communist Party.[39] It, certainly, is unlikely to restrain abuses.

In India, the institutional problems are similar:

> the state of Indian electricity sector provides a vivid reminder of how detached the sector is from adopting free market principles and the extent of distortions. Excessive energy subsidies have historically been a part of the state governments' policy program and continue to be pervasive in the state governments' operations. Subsidies for coal and petroleum products are substantial, and are significant in encouraging uneconomic use of these fuels. The length to which the state governments in India have gone to create distortions in the energy price (electricity price) is quite remarkable . . . [40]

FIGURE 2

CHEAP ABATEMENT IN THE DEVELOPING WORLD?

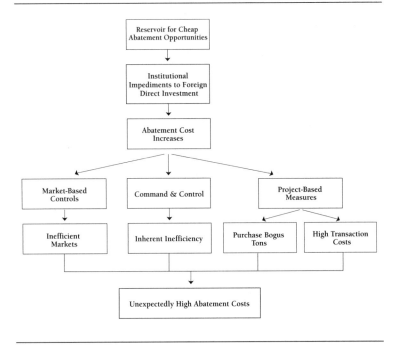

SOURCE: Author's illustration.

While both China and India have adopted important institutional reforms, both countries are likely to remain hybrid market/nonmarket regimes for decades.[41]

Hypothetically, sector-specific command-and-control approaches could substitute for market-based policies. Of course, institutionally induced limits on foreign direct investment would remain. More fundamentally, if command-and-control abatement policies are far more expensive than emissions taxes would be, abatement cost estimates that assume the use of perfectly functioning carbon taxes must be badly understating the real costs of Asian GHG reductions. This inefficiency would further erode the cost savings allegedly available from substituting Chinese and Indian GHG abatement for efforts within OECD. Figure 2 (on the previous page) illustrates some of these practical complexities.

Finally, project-based approaches would remain possible. Such projects do nothing to lift the limits on foreign direct investment or alleviate other institutional distortions. In addition, they entail high transaction costs. Many experts doubt that such projects will attain the scale needed to affect the trajectory of GHG emissions significantly.[42]

Rules for project-based GHG reductions could be loosened. Doing so would reduce transaction costs. Inevitably, though, looser controls would also allow freer-scope efforts to buy and sell cheap "anyway tons."[43] While costs would be lower, net benefits might be no higher.

For China and India, therefore, GHG abatement would be more expensive than is typically assumed. If the United States wanted to "import" abatement from these countries, the cost would substantially exceed estimates from most modeling exercises. The scale of the institutional distortions suggests that the difference between estimated abatement costs and actual ones could be large.

False Analogies

The preceding discussion provides background for an explanation of the inappropriateness of the oft-cited—but false—analogies between international GHG limits on the one hand and the WTO and the Montreal Protocol on Ozone Depleting Substances on the other. In fact, the incentives implied by international GHG controls are drastically different from those operating in WTO and the Montreal Protocol.

With GHG limits, nonparticipants typically gain, hence the appeal of free riding. Consequently, representatives of European environment ministries laboriously circle the globe wheedling, cajoling, and hectoring—seeking to expand at least the appearance of participation in Kyoto. No such efforts are needed in recruiting for the WTO. The benefits of joining the WTO club make membership much prized. Countries holding aloof from the WTO usually suffer economic losses, rather than benefiting from free-riding.

The case of Russia's ratification of Kyoto is most revealing. Europeans were compelled to buy Russia's Kyoto ratification with concessions easing the country's entry into the WTO. The example illustrates perfectly the stark difference in incentives between joining the profitable WTO businessman's club and joining the Kyoto Trappist monastery of environmentalism. Recruiting for the former is much easier than for the latter.

The WTO–Kyoto comparison is also revealing in terms of the different incentives that operate in enforcement of the two kinds of regimes. WTO members have strong egoistic incentives for punishing cheating. The WTO merely establishes the rules under which individual nations can launch retaliation for abuses. In contrast, with international GHG controls, the harm from any one nation's infringement of the rules is likely to be widely diffused among other countries. An individual nation would typically have only weak incentives to punish another's noncompliance, particularly if the transaction cost to the enforcing nation were significant. In fact, a nation punishing GHG noncompliance would actually be supplying a global public good. The logic of free riding would discourage nations from punishing noncompliance. Therefore, WTO's enforcement experience says little about the workability of enforcing a GHG control regime.

On its face, the analogy between GHG controls and the Montreal Protocol seems less far-fetched than that with the WTO. Here too, though, the analogy collapses under closer scrutiny. The Montreal agreement promised a very large surplus of benefits over costs.[44] The benefits were immediate, not delayed for many decades. The technology to replace the harmful emissions was near at hand and already under private sector development. And, in accepting the agreement, no society incurred large costs or had to impose significant lifestyle disruptions on its populace.

Even with all these relative advantages, Montreal's success was not a foregone conclusion. Clearly, though, the problem of ozone-depleting substances is very different from that of GHG controls. And the scale of its difficulty is far smaller. Hence, Montreal's success says almost nothing about the prospects for international GHG controls.

Conclusion

Kyoto's environmental ineffectuality seems incurable. GHG controls will not produce enough technological innovation to enable aggressive emissions cuts. While climate change may prove more costly than expected, institutional considerations suggest that GHG abatement will also be unexpectedly expensive. Given these high costs, adopting GHG controls is not in China's or India's national self-interest. Nor, considering the institutional problems inherent in the Chinese and Indian economies, is it likely to be in America's interest to pay them to abate. The analogies sometimes cited to defend the claim that effective international GHG controls might succeed after all prove, on closer inspection, false and misleading.

Thus, the conditions required for a successful international GHG limitation agreement appear to be absent. If so, the problem with Kyoto runs deeper than the agreement's mechanics. Tinkering with its targets or architecture cannot remedy the entire venture's deeper unreality.

The conclusion that international GHG controls are, at least for the foreseeable future, beyond reach has profound consequences for domestic climate policy. The theory behind domestic GHG controls has always been that the American system would form a bridge to an eventual international control regime. If no such international regime seems likely to emerge, domestic controls could become a bridge to nowhere. The next chapter will discuss the Bush administration's treatment of domestic controls and its proposed alternatives to them.

3

Bush Administration Domestic Climate Policy

President Bush has rejected calls for a domestic GHG cap-and-trade program, although not quite as decisively as he has rebuffed Kyoto. Powerful political factors urged this course of action. For any administration, domestic GHG controls would entail many political disadvantages. The Bush administration, especially before the president's reelection, had especially strong motives for shunning such proposals.

As with Kyoto, the administration's opposition has not killed domestic cap-and-trade proposals. At the state level, proposals continue to advance, and there is some risk that these plans will set baleful precedents for eventual GHG limits at the federal level. Ultimately, the federal courts could decide the fate of state-level GHG limits.

Meanwhile, the Bush administration strategy has substituted an alternative package for cap-and-trade containing technology policies, voluntary controls by industry, and some sector-specific regulatory approaches. Of these proposals, only the R&D initiatives might contribute significantly to climate policy success.

Unfortunately, the implementation of the administration's R&D program suffers from important deficiencies. It excludes valuable areas like adaptation and geoengineering. It focuses too heavily on making largely incremental changes to a rather narrow set of technologies. And the quest for climate-change solutions seems to play only a secondary role in determining R&D funding priorities.

The President's Rejection of Domestic GHG Cap-and-Trade

As a presidential candidate in 2000, George W. Bush endorsed GHG cap-and-trade for the electric power sector. In March 2001, he reversed this position, a decision precipitated by a letter from four Republican senators.[1] Since then, the president has resisted all proposals for domestic GHG cap-and-trade programs.

In announcing his opposition to mandatory domestic GHG controls, President Bush proclaimed that the current policy should be reviewed in 2012. At that point, if the current policy's results are unsatisfactory and the science warrants further actions, he said, the United States "may" adopt broad-based mandatory controls.[2] The equivocal wording combined with a policy review date four years beyond the president's maximum tenure in office attenuated the resonance of this commitment.

Bush has read Michael Crichton's science fiction novel, *State of Fear*. In the book, Crichton argues that global climate change is an unproven theory, and that the threat is grossly exaggerated. Bush was obviously impressed. In late 2005, Karl Rove arranged for Bush to meet with Crichton. The two "talked for an hour and were in near-total agreement."[3] At other times, though, the president has said he regards climate change as a real problem. To the outside observer, Bush's reported reaction to Crichton seems at odds with his protestations of serious concern about climate change.

President Bush's ambivalence—if that is what it is—is hardly unprecedented. Most presidents are likely to engage domestic GHG controls reluctantly at best. As a political task, enacting domestic cap-and-trade offers daunting difficulties and few political rewards. The Clinton administration shrank from it, preferring to temporize with protracted Kyoto negotiations.

Many characteristics of climate change are likely to repel most political entrepreneurs. Specifically, the explicit harm from climate change lies far in the future; as University of Toronto political science professor Thomas Homer-Dixon has observed, "Human-induced greenhouse warming will probably develop over many decades and may not have truly serious implications for humankind for a half century or more after the signal is first detected."[4] Yet to stabilize atmospheric concentrations at low levels, the initial costs of mitigation must be incurred early.

In effect, climate-change mitigation requires a wealth transfer from current generations to future ones. Experience with Social Security reform highlights just how difficult such transfers are for democratic political institutions. The electorate understandably distrusts office-seekers' claims that their policies will produce future gain in excess of present pain. Voters are typically unable and unwilling to conduct deep policy analysis assessing the validity of such promises.

Office-seekers rightly anticipate that the electorate will see the near-term costs yet heavily discount promises of future benefits. Supporting such causes is usually not conducive to electoral success. Public opinion data confirm that, as an issue, climate change lacks strong political appeal. The public is aware of the issue and supports government action, but the level of understanding or concern is low.[5]

Consistent with the problem's apparent temporal remoteness, the public accords climate change a low priority. In general, most Americans do not worry much about environmental issues.[6] And even among environmental issues, climate change occasions comparatively little concern. The most recent Gallup poll on the environment showed that the public ranked climate change seventh on a list of ten environmental concerns.[7]

The public's blasé response to climate change has withstood many assaults. Former Vice President Al Gore remains a passionate and relentlessly vocal advocate of action on climate change. Hollywood has produced two sensationalistic disaster movies on the subject. For a while, the news media trumpeted a Pentagon "worst case" analysis. The Turner Foundation spent $10 million a few years ago in an campaign designed to enflame public anxiety about climate change. These efforts came to nothing. Only a small increase in concern has emerged, despite environmental groups' current, more sustained grassroots efforts.[8]

Beyond the climate change problem's politically off-putting features, the solution also clashes with the dictates of conventional political entrepreneurship. The revealed preference of much of the

American public is for a low-population-density settlement pattern. This preference is now embodied in housing patterns, automobiles, public infrastructure, commercial buildings, and durable goods of all kinds. Government policies that would increase the costs of driving would diminish the value of much of the capital stock. Not surprisingly, Americans expect their government to maintain the low gasoline prices needed to sustain this settlement pattern and the capital stocks that embody it. For this reason, gasoline is the most politically sensitive commodity price in America.[9] Even Democratic politicians who express strong concern about climate change also affirm their desire to control the cost of gasoline.

The owners of that capital are a formidable political force. The Clinton administration's BTU tax fiasco confirmed the intense unpopularity of energy-tax proposals. Bipartisan criticism of the Bush administration's failure to halt fuel price increases reaffirms the lesson.

Stringent GHG cap-and-trade plans would collide head-on with this political reality. Such plans work by boosting energy price levels and changing relative prices among fuels. In particular, an economy-wide GHG proposal would certainly increase gasoline prices. It is little wonder that such proposals are more popular with journalists and academics than with practicing politicians.

Comprehensive GHG controls would also increase other politically sensitive energy prices, presenting their opponents with powerful allies. Extractive industries (coal, oil, natural gas) are formidable players in the policymaking process. Natural gas is a key feedstock for the chemical and fertilizer industries. In general, agriculture is energy-intensive. Traditionally, farmers denounce as hideous injustice any policy that increases their production costs (or requires them to bear a larger share of them). Cement production is an important source of GHG emissions, with implications for the construction and highway sectors. The poor pay a higher percentage of their income for energy; their advocates will protest measures that would increase that burden.

Opposition also encompasses regional politics. The South, for instance, meets its very high summer air conditioning needs with coal-fired electricity, making this region especially vulnerable to the

costs of GHG controls. Coal production is disproportionately important to some state economies. Agriculture, an energy intensive sector,
is concentrated in the Great Plains.

If politically united, these regional and sectoral interests are powerful enough to defeat legislation to boost energy prices. In response,
as was the case with the Clinton BTU tax proposal, proponents of
higher energy prices typically grant exemptions to split the opposition. That tactic may work, depending on how artfully it is done, but
it is risky. Once exemptions begin, there is no obvious stopping place.
The proposal may quickly degenerate into an arbitrary and ineffectual patchwork. At that point, even if something is enacted, the
purpose is largely defeated.

To all appearances, this legislative deconstruction process is
already at work with GHG cap-and-trade proposals. The McCain-
Lieberman cap-and-trade bill, for example, exempted agriculture and
home heating oil. High use of home heating oil in New England
makes proposals to increase the price of this commodity a political
taboo, despite that region's pretensions to environmental virtue. Any
politician from that area, or one expecting to compete in the New
Hampshire presidential primary, must shun violation of it. And the
exemptions were just the drafters' proposal; before any bill could
have been enacted, additional concessions would surely have been
made to other interests.

Beyond these general considerations, President Bush has had specific reasons for eschewing involvement with GHG cap-and-trade
proposals. In addition to his sporadic doubts about the importance
of climate change, he has other urgent priorities that urge him to con-
sign climate policy to a relatively low rank on his political agenda—
and, by and large, he has.

The California energy crisis, the events of 9/11 and the war in
Iraq, the blackout in the Northeast, and the hurricanes of 2005
with their concomitant rise in natural gas, oil, and gasoline prices,
continue to push climate policy far down the Bush administration's
agenda. It is no accident that the high point of public prominence
for climate policy came during the Clinton administration. Falling
between the Cold War and the current conflict, that administration

took a "holiday from history"—the ideal political environment for climate policy. And even then, of course, we have nothing to show for its efforts.

Human beings are "attention misers."[10] The tumultuous events of the Bush presidency have intensified the competition for the spotlight. After 9/11, war and recession largely monopolized public and governmental attention. Polling data show that in this period, climate change lost ground in the battle for public attention.[11] Even after the economic recovery, concern remains well below its (none-too-high) 2000 levels.[12] Only a comparatively few issues can be prominent at any one time:

> There is a limit on the capacity of the system to process a multitude of agenda items. . . . A real perceived problem has a solution available, and there is no political barrier to action. But these subjects queue up for the available decision-making time, and pressing items crowd the less pressing ones down in the queue.[13]

For the general public, climate change was one of the issues that 9/11 and our series of energy "crises" definitely crowded down in the queue. The president has been under little or no domestic political pressure to deal with it.

The president's own management style has amplified the temptation to relegate climate policy to insignificance. This administration focuses its resources on a relatively few high-priority issues, of which climate is never going to be one. As a second- or third-tier issue, it receives less presidential attention than has been the case in some previous presidencies.[14]

Electoral considerations reinforce this management style. For example, less than 5 percent of voters typically say that environmental issues were the most important determinant of their votes in national elections.[15]

Environment, moreover, is a political "market niche" in which President Bush has chosen to compete only minimally. This decision was sensible in the context of the president's reelection strategy, which was based on mobilizing the Republican electoral base. Statistically, Republicans are less concerned about the environment than other voters. In an early 2006 poll, 51 percent of self-described Democrats and 41 percent of independents said that they worried a great deal about the environment. Only 26 percent of Republicans agreed.[16]

On climate change, the partisan divide is even starker. Of Democrats, 49 percent worry a great deal. Of independents, the figure is 38 percent. Only 16 percent of Republicans say they worry greatly about climate change.[17] Emphasizing climate change would not support the president's electoral focus on the mobilization of the Republican base.

Electoral College considerations also reinforced the logic of ceding the climate issue. George Bush won West Virginia with a pro-coal agenda. Indeed, the president depended heavily on coal-producing and consuming regions like the South, the upper Midwest, the Great Plains, and the intermountain West. Stringent GHG limits would damage these regions economically. Climate policy concerns, if they resonate at all, do so primarily in states that voted against the president, although Florida may be (a somewhat ambiguous) counterexample.

The Bush campaigns also received large contributions from fossil-fuel producers. Regardless of the president's stance on climate policy, his campaign could have out-competed its Democratic rivals for this money. But it is only natural in politics for the concerns of major political donors to reach the ears of candidates, and, at least according to the private comments of some former executive branch employees, the pleas of some of the president's important oil and gas industry campaign contributors played a significant role in reversing his position on GHG cap-and-trade.

With little to gain politically from endorsing GHG limits, the president has sought to undermine support for mandatory GHG controls. Active overt opposition to congressionally initiated GHG limits exposes the president to criticism for being excessively probusiness. Such proposals mobilize the Democrats' green constituents while they sow dissent among Republican legislators.

The Continuing Progress of Domestic Cap-and-Trade

Notwithstanding the president's staunch opposition, domestic cap-and-trade proposals continue to advance. At the federal level, such plans proliferate, and several states have also spawned them.

The president's steadfast resistance to GHG cap-and-trade limits has yielded some benefits. For example, it appears to have gradually dampened the ambitiousness of congressional cap-and-trade proposals. As a general rule, the marginal abatement costs of successive bills have been declining. These include the Jeffords Bill, which was the first center of congressional attention in 2001. McCain-Lieberman was the next dominant bill in 2003, with a less expensive version emerging later. The Bingaman Bill, introduced in 2005, incorporated a so-called safety valve, making it more cost-effective. And new legislation proposed in 2006 by congressmen Udall and Petri (H.R. 5049), if it gains prominence, would continue this trend. True, the traditional supporters of the older, more draconian controls continue to reintroduce bills of that type. But gentler, more cost-effective, price-based controls have increasingly emerged as the only kind of bill able to garner centrist Republican support, which is essential for any legislation to be viable.

While this legislative evolution has ground slowly forward, the nation has escaped the costs of cap-and-trade—and lost the benefits. Determining the net effect depends on assumptions about the quality of whatever cap-and-trade program might have been enacted had the president favored it.

The congressional impasse on GHG controls has also caused some collateral damage. For example, it has prevented enactment of the administration's Clear Skies legislation, which would have been a cost-beneficial step towards cleaner air (with modest GHG reduction benefits as well). Its defeat is a net loss.

A second harmful effect has been the sparking of a state-level movement for GHG cap-and-trade programs. Several northeastern governors are trying to impose GHG limits on power plants operating within their states; similar ideas are circulating on the West Coast. Most important, California recently enacted a stringent regulatory plan for limiting GHG emissions. In theory, this plan will return the state to 1990 emissions levels by 2020. The law's actual implications remain unclear, with most of the key details left to be decided by regulatory agencies. Insofar as it is possible to tell, the policy mechanisms of the California law are a throwback to costly command-and-control approaches. Aggressive targets combined with inefficient implementation are likely to entail very high costs. Whether the state will persevere as the real costs of the legislation become more apparent is a matter of speculation at this point.[18]

Regional idiosyncrasies may allow state-level proposals to succeed at least temporarily. Many regions, such as New England, California, and the Pacific Northwest, evince above-average levels of concern about climate change. Typically, these regions are net electricity importers. In other cases, they rely disproportionately on fuels other than coal. In themselves, therefore, these state or regional limits could be viewed as merely "feel-good" environmentalism, imposing controls where emissions are already low.

The proponents of state-level controls intend them to lead to national-level legislation. They hope that numerous separate state measures will cause chaos for the regulated industries, which, they calculate, will respond by demanding federal preemption. This strategy, however, brings risks. It may, for example, set unfortunate precedents that will degrade the cost-effectiveness of the subsequent national control plans. At least two potential threats of this kind are already apparent.

First, for administrative reasons, state-level cap-and-trade programs can only cover power plants. Such sector-specific controls charge a price for GHG emissions from power plants while charging nothing for comparable emissions from other sources. Unavoidably, this strategy misses some low-cost abatement opportunities, driving up the cost of achieving any given level of emissions cuts. The precedent is hardly an appealing one for national legislation.[19]

Second, the states most likely to adopt GHG controls are those that will also most probably adopt Kyoto-style hard caps. In general, only the most environmentally conscious states—those with the strongest green pressure groups—would disadvantage their economies with

GHG limits. And those groups are passionate advocates of Kyoto-style quantitative (rather than price-based) GHG caps. If state plans are the model for eventual federal legislation, that template is likely to embody the worst features of the Kyoto system.

To keep a balanced perspective, one should also consider that the green pressure groups' strategy of forcing federal action by enacting state-level controls might still fail. Indeed, it could backfire. Because these groups demand steep, near-term emission cuts, the state plans they seek to impose are likely to be expensive; practical experience with those costs may dissuade would-be imitators. And efforts to cut those costs may undermine the effectiveness of the programs. One possible market response to regional cap-and-trade would be merely to import more power from neighboring areas without controls. In principle, emissions could even rise. In any case, the resulting leakage will certainly harm the program's cost-effectiveness.

State-level cap-and-trade plans could also die in the courts. The regulated industries argue that these plans encroach on the president's power to conduct international negotiations on climate policy and conflict with congressional prerogatives.[20] At this point, one can only speculate that should the courts strike down these state initiatives, the wide-ranging legislative campaigns will have been political theater, full of sound and fury but signifying nothing.

The Bush Administration's Alternative to Domestic Cap-and-Trade

Legal and legislative battles continue to swirl around domestic GHG cap-and-trade proposals. So far, the Bush administration's opposition appears unshaken. At least for the remainder of President Bush's tenure in office, it is likely he will be able to prevent implementation of any federal GHG cap-and-trade program. But the administration's climate policy has not been merely passive.

The administration's domestic climate policy parallels its international one. It has created an alternative to domestic cap-and-trade; once again, technology is the centerpiece. Figure 3 illustrates the management structure of the administration's entire climate change effort.

FIGURE 3

CABINET-LEVEL ENGAGEMENT IN CLIMATE CHANGE POLIC

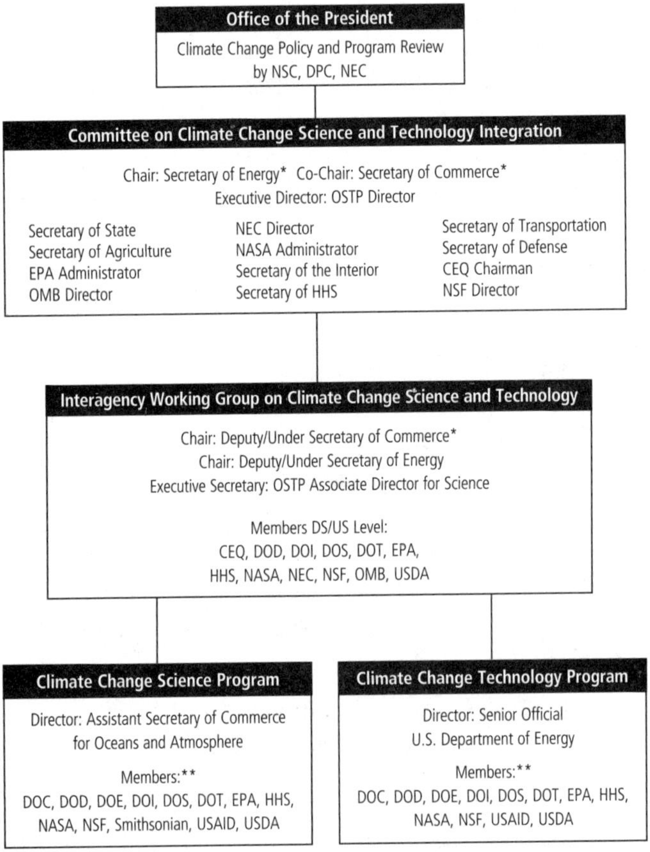

Office of the President
Climate Change Policy and Program Review
by NSC, DPC, NEC

Committee on Climate Change Science and Technology Integration

Chair: Secretary of Energy* Co-Chair: Secretary of Commerce*
Executive Director: OSTP Director

Secretary of State	NEC Director	Secretary of Transportation
Secretary of Agriculture	NASA Administrator	Secretary of Defense
EPA Administrator	Secretary of the Interior	CEQ Chairman
OMB Director	Secretary of HHS	NSF Director

Interagency Working Group on Climate Change Science and Technology

Chair: Deputy/Under Secretary of Commerce*
Chair: Deputy/Under Secretary of Energy
Executive Secretary: OSTP Associate Director for Science

Members DS/US Level:
CEQ, DOD, DOI, DOS, DOT, EPA,
HHS, NASA, NEC, NSF, OMB, USDA

Climate Change Science Program

Director: Assistant Secretary of Commerce
for Oceans and Atmosphere

Members:**
DOC, DOD, DOE, DOI, DOS, DOT, EPA, HHS,
NASA, NSF, Smithsonian, USAID, USDA

Climate Change Technology Program

Director: Senior Official
U.S. Department of Energy

Members:**
DOC, DOD, DOE, DOI, DOS, DOT, EPA, HHS,
NASA, NSF, USAID, USDA

---

*Chair and Vice Chair of Committee and Working Group alternate annually.   **CEQ, OSTP, and OMB also participate.

SOURCE: Based on the CCTP Strategic Plan, figures 1-1, 1-4.

FIGURE 4
BUSH ADMINISTRATION DOMESTIC CLIMATE CHANGE INITIATIVES

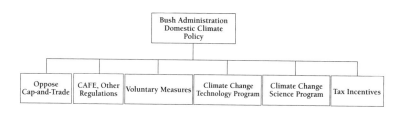

SOURCE: Author's illustration.

The resulting policy has many components. As Harlan Watson, the Department of State's chief negotiator on climate change, has explained:

> Addressing the challenge of global climate change will require a sustained long-term commitment by all nations over many generations. To this end, the President has established a robust and flexible climate change policy that harnesses the power of markets and technological innovation, maintains economic growth, and encourages global participation. Major elements of this approach include implementing near-term policies and measures to slow the growth in greenhouse gas emissions, advancing climate change science, accelerating climate change technology development, and promoting international collaboration.[21]

Admittedly, my separation of these initiatives into domestic and international is somewhat arbitrary; the administration's climate policy clearly reflects a unified strategic vision. Figure 4 (above) summarizes the administration's major domestic initiatives, just as the international climate initiatives are summarized in figure 1.

President Bush has said, "Our approach [to climate change] must be consistent with the long-term goal of stabilizing greenhouse gas concentrations in the atmosphere."[22] However, as already noted, the president also seems ambivalent about the importance of climate change and the scientific evidence of human influence upon it. Thus, he qualified his remarks about stabilizing atmospheric concentrations with the valid caveat that science had not yet indicated what atmospheric concentrations were safe.[23] Given the scientific uncertainties, the administration argues, a more precise policy would inherently be an arbitrary one.

The Climate Change Science Program (CCSP) has the mission of narrowing the scientific uncertainties. The CCSP is charged with coordinating and setting priorities for the government's diverse efforts to advance climate science. Managed through a multi-agency committee, it has had an annual budget of about $2 billion.

Critics are unimpressed. Few oppose the search for better scientific knowledge. But many protest that there is already sufficient knowledge to justify action to retard climate change. At least outside Europe, as a matter of practical politics, that assertion appears to go too far. As already mentioned, large doubts persist about the scale, timing, geographical distribution, and economic consequences of climate change. Some of these questions relate to demography, economics, and technology. Some relate to science.

For example, mathematical models of the earth's climate are critically important to the case for climate change mitigation. These models simulate atmospheric, marine, biological, and social systems and the linkages among them. Yet most omit important scientific relationships—often for reasons of computational economy. Perhaps as a result, none of the current linked ocean atmosphere models can accurately simulate current global climate without arbitrary adjustments.[24] Noting the resulting scientific uncertainties, a recent commentator observed:

> These complexities might not be so troublesome if greenhouse gases were a minor byproduct of the modern economy, but they are not. Unlike lead or chlorofluorocarbons, whose control was relatively easy, reducing greenhouse gas emissions will require substantial changes

in social organization, impacting all nations and all economic sectors, threatening substantial economic costs,
and stirring rancorous controversy over the distribution
of the burden.[25]

Given the economic stakes, proponents of GHG controls bear an
exceptionally high burden of proof. So far, the scientific foundation
of the case for action has been too weak to motivate changes of the
scale required to halt global climate change.

While the CCSP seeks to resolve the continuing scientific uncertainties, the Bush administration's Climate Change Technology
Program (CCTP) aims to reduce the costs of reducing GHG emissions. This program is supposed to coordinate the government's
diverse climate-related technology development initiatives to better
set priorities among these programs.[26] While it is also managed by
an interagency committee, more than 85 percent of the funding it
oversees resides in the Department of Energy.

The CCTP is primarily a R&D program. It is the one Bush administration climate policy initiative that could profoundly affect the
prospects of long-term global GHG emissions. Hence, the next section of this chapter is devoted to evaluating it.

Beyond these R&D initiatives, the rest of the Bush administration
domestic climate policy is variegated. Many programs are voluntary,
and a number of them are oriented toward technology diffusion.
EPA's "Methane to Markets" program is one example. The administration has also revised and (most would say) strengthened a voluntary registry for GHG reductions authorized by Congress in 1992.
The registering of reductions might entitle firms to free emissions
allowances or establish a baseline for measuring progress in some
future mandatory cap-and-trade program.

The administration rejected a mandatory registry, the implementation of which would have created a dangerous precedent. It would have
established an expectation that a future mandatory GHG control program would be implemented "downstream," at the point of emissions.[27]
Indeed, according to David Conover, who managed the program, even
proposals to institute a voluntary registry sparked contention.[28]

An upstream system, applied at the point at which fossil fuel enters the stream of commerce, would be easier to administer and, consequently, more efficient. A downstream system would face the impossible challenge of enforcing controls on countless small sources. Necessarily, it would exempt these small sources, compromising the system's comprehensiveness and uniformity. The Bush administration's rejection of the mandatory registry is, therefore, a useful contribution to improving the design of future mandatory cap-and-trade proposals.[29]

The administration is also implementing various small regulatory initiatives, notably raising corporate average fuel economy (CAFE) standards and promulgating efficiency standards for appliances and other energy-consuming equipment. An early proposal raised standards on SUVs and light trucks. In the spring of 2006, the administration asked Congress to give it authority to reform and strengthen CAFE standards for automobiles.

Increasing CAFE standards is a particularly inefficient and costly way to reduce GHG emissions.[30] CAFE proposals, though, serve the politically popular (although largely specious and unrealistic) cause of achieving "energy independence."[31]

The administration's CAFE policy appears to contradict its proclaimed opposition to mandatory GHG limits. The administration also acquiesced to several new appliance and building efficiency standards in the 2005 energy legislation. For an administration that is presumably concerned about cost-effectiveness, all these command-and-control regulations seem an odd expedient. Nonetheless, these CAFE regulations and other efficiency standards are small-bore policies. Consequently, the proposals' costs are small, even if their benefits are smaller still.

The administration's stance makes tactical sense. To more conservative constituencies, CAFE increases can be publicly justified by references to energy security rather than to climate change. Moreover, in the aftermath of energy price hikes, raising CAFE standards will not cause immediate economic harm. CAFE was initially enacted after the oil price hikes of the 1970s; at that time, it simply legally formalized market changes already in progress.[32] The economic harm occurred later, when oil prices fell in the 1980s. At that point, the standards actually began preventing auto manufacturers from selling the kinds of vehicles that consumers wanted most. The Bush administration CAFE increases will presumably be as harmless as those in the late 1970s—unless fuel prices plummet again.

Even in that case, the lost profits and sacrificed consumer satisfaction will be nearly invisible. And the culprits will have left office. Meanwhile, sufficiently audacious administration officials can claim to have struck a blow against climate change. For the moment, they have paid no economic price for these bragging rights.

The administration has established a symbolic national target of reducing the GHG intensity of the American economy by four percentage points below the recent historical trend line. Some analysts see this symbolic goal as yielding useful consequences:

> The emphasis on mitigation moves away from a policy focused solely on science and technology. The goal of 4 percent reductions from forecast emissions levels in 10 years is within the range of economically sensible near-term targets. An intensity approach draws attention to the importance of balancing economic and environmental concerns. And the transferable credit system could be the beginning of a tradable permit system and encourage institutions to deal with sequestration and fugitive emissions.[33]

Other analysts reach opposite conclusions. They point out seemingly irrational implications of the intensity approach. Rapid economic growth implies a relaxation of abatement. Recession calls for its escalation.[34] Perhaps more to the point, the target is a mere wish.

Assessing the Domestic Technology Programs

For the federal government, R&D is often part of the response to any new problem:

> Federal support to basic and applied research and for the creation of research facilities has a long history in this

country. No other nation has remotely as successful an enterprise, and our practices are a model for the rest of the world. The hallmark of the US approach is project selection according to merit, and, in general, flexibility in accommodating education as an important byproduct of funded research activity. The successful government manager in an agency that fosters technology creation is knowledgeable about advances in the field and attentive to outside expert opinion; direct support of R&D projects is the manager's major tool.[35]

Thus, it is no surprise that the Bush administration would rely heavily on R&D as a central component of its response to climate change. But that decision brings the administration's climate policy into conflict with an array of institutional problems. Some of these problems are generic; they are present in all government-funded R&D, or at least in government-funded energy R&D. Others are specific to the politics and organizational setting of the administration's climate-related R&D program, the Climate Change Technology Program.

Let's first consider the generic R&D problems. It seems fair to observe that the federal government has not been equally successful in all of its R&D ventures over the years. Typically, particularly in the energy field, government has been better at developing new technologies than at encouraging their deployment. And its basic and applied research efforts have performed better than many of its demonstration projects.[36]

The federal government is prone to launching demonstration projects prematurely. These projects are started before the technologies are ready in part because they are attractive as pork barrel politics. And short congressional electoral cycles encourage imprudent haste. In general, an impatient attitude toward government R&D seems almost rooted in the Constitution.

The problematic nature of energy demonstration projects is a classic example of a generic problem of government-funded R&D that may have an especially troubling application for climate-related

R&D. None of the technologies that might someday make major contributions to solving the climate problem is yet close to being economically competitive. Carbon capture and storage (CCS) technologies are a good example. Today, most estimates suggest that new power plants built around the best available CCS technology might capture and store carbon at a cost of perhaps $100 per ton, but no knowledgeable political observer believes the United States will be willing to enact GHG controls at anything like this level of stringency.

Demonstration projects are likely to demonstrate primarily that climate-related technologies are not yet ready for commercialization. In some cases, such as wind power, the technology has been commercialized but is still not competitive, and, even in the long term, it is likely to remain too small-scale to be of much value. The raison d'être of climate-related demonstration projects should be to show that the technologies are both close to commercialization and have the potential to generate large-scale emissions reductions. It is hard to see what current technologies meet both of these criteria.

Pouring resources into big demonstration projects reduces the funding available for the smaller-scale, earlier phases of R&D on more promising technologies. Many such technologies exist, yet the federal government often does not foster their development.[37] It is likely that at least some of the large sums of money being spent on CCS, and most of what is spent on wind, could be better spent on the early development of more innovative technologies.

The Energy Policy Act of 2005 (EPA 2005) may have exacerbated this misallocation of resources. It expanded authorization for climate-related technology development, potentially increasing the total size of the climate-related R&D effort. How much of this increased spending will actually materialize is questionable; congressional appropriations committees have the final say. Congress also created a plethora of tax incentives in the EPA 2005, which will supposedly encourage the diffusion of "climate-friendly" technologies. The Clinton administration had (largely unsuccessfully) proposed similar policies. Those proposals were shown to be very cost-ineffective.[38]

Tax incentives of this kind can be politically popular. Their industrial beneficiaries naturally like them, but they are typically very expensive compared to funding earlier stages of technology development. They also encourage the costly lock-in of inferior technologies at the expense of better ones that are not yet sufficiently developed.[39] Thus, a prominent EPA 2005 tax subsidy lavishly rewarded buyers of large hybrid cars and trucks. The administration, although it opposed some of the 2005 act's tax subsidies, seems not to have assessed how this use of funds compared in cost-effectiveness with comparable increases in government R&D, or in light of the lock-in risks inherent in deployment subsidies.

The CCTP also employs more direct R&D funding routes. A critically important instrument of climate policy, it seeks to foster progress on a broad spectrum of technologies, including hydrogen vehicles, end-use efficiency, renewables, nuclear power, fusion, carbon capture and sequestration, and improvements to the power grid. The work encompasses activities from basic science to deployment. Table 1 on the following page summarizes the CCTP's major components.

The CCTP's components cost slightly less than $3 billion annually. The program's scale is certainly substantial. Conversely, the task of producing the multiple technological revolutions needed to curb anthropogenic climate change is very large compared to CCTP's expenditures. Several specifics of CCTP's strategy are constructive and important. For example, the Bush administration shifted the emphasis in automotive technology from near-term mileage improvements to longer-term consideration of more radical innovations, such as hydrogen vehicles of various types. Although the prospects for such vehicles remain uncertain, as do those for developing GHG-free hydrogen sources, the move to a longer-run, more revolutionary focus comports with the logic of the climate change challenge. It is also more consistent with the optimal division of labor between public- and private-sector R&D.

The president's 2006 State of the Union message highlighted the potential for use of biofuels. The concept has political appeal; it promises, in theory, to decrease gasoline prices and boost farm income. Bioengineering breakthroughs could, in principle, enhance the attractiveness of this technology.[40] On the other hand, skeptics

TABLE 1

MAJOR COMPONENTS OF THE CLIMATE CHANGE TECHNOLOGY PROGRAM

Agency	Selected Examples of Climate Change–Related Technology R&D Activities
DOC	Instrumentation, Standards, Ocean Sequestration, Decision Support Tools
DOD	Aircraft, Engines, Fuels, Trucks, Equipment, Power, Fuel Cells, Lasers, Energy Management, Basic Research
DOE	Energy Efficiency, Renewable Energy, Nuclear Fission and Fusion, Fossil Fuels and Power, Carbon Sequestration, Basic Energy Sciences, Hydrogen, Bio-Fuels, Electric Grid and Infrastructure
DOI	Land, Forest, and Prairie Management, Mining, Sequestration, Geothermal, Terrestrial Sequestration Technology Development
DOS*	International Science and Technology Cooperation, Oceans, Environment
DOT	Aviation, Highways, Rail, Freight, Maritime, Urban Mass Transit, Transportation Systems, Efficiency and Safety
EPA	Mitigation of CO_2 and Non-CO_2 GHG Emissions through Voluntary Partnership Programs, including Energy STAR, Climate Leaders, Green Power, Combined Heat and Power, State and Local Clean Energy, Methane and High-GWP Gases, and Transportation; GHG Emissions Inventory
HHS*	Environmental Sciences, Biotechnology, Genome Sequencing, Health Effects
NASA	Earth Observations, Measuring, Monitoring, Aviation Equipment, Operations and Infrastructure Efficiency
NSF	Geosciences, Oceans, Nanoscale Science and Engineering, Computational Sciences
USAID*	International Assistance, Technology Deployment, Land Use, Human Impacts
USDA	Carbon Fluxes in Soils, Forests and Other Vegetation, Carbon Sequestration, Nutrient Management, Cropping Systems, Forest and Forest Products Management, Livestock, and Waste Management, Biomass Energy and Bio-based Products Development

* CCTP-related funding for the indicated agencies is not included in the totals for CCTP in the budget tables of Appendix A of The Plan. However, the agencies participate in CCTP R&D planning and coordination as members of CCTP's Working Groups. Agency titles for the acronyms above are shown in Appendix A.

SOURCE: Based on the CCTP Strategic Plan, tables 1-1, 1-6.

argue that the land and water requirements of biofuels will limit their usefulness as a large-scale GHG abatement technology.[41]

In theory, the project's management will assess the potential contributions of these programs to the goals of climate policy. By feeding these assessments into the budget process, CCTP will supposedly improve the cost-effectiveness of government R&D as a source of future climate solutions.

The CCTP's recently released draft strategic plan lays out a hierarchy of vision, mission, strategic goals, core approaches, and a prioritization process. It offers a scenario-analysis that illustrates some potential choices, and it assesses contributions R&D might make to reducing the cost of combating climate change. Clearly, much valid and valuable thought has gone into the plan. No other nation has prepared a similar one. Following up on its publication, CCTP management conducted a series of expert workshops, bringing together individuals with a diverse mix of technical and scientific expertise to look for gaps and omissions within the draft strategic plan—an indication of management commitment to continuing improvement in the CCTP planning process.

Notwithstanding the CCTP's many virtues, problems abound, and they are serious. Broadly considered, three technology strategies are available for dealing with climate change. First, technological progress can lower the cost of GHG abatement; the CCTP focuses on this goal. Second, technology can enable what is called geoengineering, the use of technologies that would avoid harmful climate change while allowing emissions. (Among other options, geoengineering could involve increasing earth's albedo to offset the warming effects of rising GHG concentrations.) Third, technological innovation could aid adaptation to climate change. Technologies like heat- and drought-resistant crops, stockpiling genetic material from endangered species, or hydrological projects that minimize the costs of rising sea levels can minimize the costs of the climate change that is already inevitable.

Currently, the CCTP is entirely focused on just the first of those three options, climate change mitigation; in fact, the program explicitly excludes R&D on geoengineering and adaptation.[42] This choice, which is potentially of great significance, does not appear to have received an appropriate level of scrutiny. To underscore this point, one recommendation of the expert workshops described above was to expand the program's agenda to include geoengineering.[43]

Some mix of the three technology strategies is most likely to meet the goal of minimizing the sum of the costs of climate change and the costs of countermeasures taken against it—the definition of an optimal climate policy. The CCTP should develop the suite of technologies best able to implement this cost-minimizing strategy. Each of the two strategies presently missing is, in fact, crucially important to overall success.

Adaptation can significantly reduce net damages from climate change. More recent damage estimates typically fall below those of earlier ones because recent studies have better accounted for adaptation.[44] The evident power of adaptation to decrease damages suggests using R&D to boost that power. As Harvard economist Richard Cooper has observed, adaptation

> means *inter alia* pushing ahead with both the basic science and applications of genetic engineering in many areas, especially agriculture, but also to provide potential substitutes for possible useful species that may be lost. That could be supplemented by a systematic program for collecting, cataloguing, and storing genetic material, mainly but not exclusively from plants, in the form of seed banks and DNA.[45]

Taken one step further, the logic of adaptation implies conducting R&D on geoengineering. Climate policy must cope with the possibility of low-probability but high-cost events.[46] Should the climate system manifest a large and harmful discontinuity, having a mechanism for "scramming" the climate change process could prove invaluable.[47] Indeed, unless we are prepared to assign a zero probability to "nasty surprises" from climate change, there seems good reason to undertake such research.[48] As one prominent group of scholars has explained,

Geoengineering in the climate change context refers mainly to altering the planetary radiation balance to affect climate and uses technologies to compensate for the inadvertent global warming produced by fossil fuel CO_2 and other greenhouse gases. An early idea was to put layers of reflective sulfate aerosol in the upper atmosphere to counteract greenhouse warming. Variations on the sunblocking theme include injecting sub-micrometer dust to the stratosphere in shells fired by naval guns, increasing cloud cover by seeding, and shadowing earth by objects in space. . . . Climate model runs indicate that the spatial pattern of climate would resemble that without fossil fuel CO_2. Engineering the optical properties of aerosols injected to the stratosphere to produce a variety of climate effects has also been proposed.[49]

The natural analogue of this "scram" button, large volcanic eruptions, can powerfully affect global temperature. In the year following the Mount Pinatubo eruption, global mean temperature fell by .6°C. This experience suggests an opportunity. From the standpoint of achieving global cooling, volcanoes are very inefficient. The particles they expel are too big, and most do not reach sufficient altitude. A more optimal injection of particles into the atmosphere could accomplish a larger temperature change with a much smaller mass of particles.[50]

As insurance against runaway climate change, research on geoengineering may be superior to attempting to reach consensus on how to achieve rapid emissions cuts. Because mitigation is so slow, it must be initiated many decades before science confirms the danger of rapid climate change. Realistically, political consensus is impossible under these circumstances, as the Kyoto experience is demonstrating.

Geoengineering, in contrast, could be implemented swiftly. For one thing, reaching international agreement for geoengineering would be relatively easy, at least compared to global emissions reductions. Such an agreement would be about the sharing of monetary costs, a type of negotiation with which we have much experience.[51] In the meantime, the costs would be confined to the R&D needed to demonstrate the technology's feasibility.

Moreover, the deployment of geoengineering technology may be inexpensive compared to draconian emission cuts. The U.S. National Academies of Sciences, after studying geoengineering, concluded, "Perhaps one of the surprises of this analysis is the relatively low cost at which some of the geoengineering options might be implemented."[52]

Finally, geoengineering is more consistent with individual liberty than are GHG controls. Geoengineering would require no government-imposed lifestyle changes. For the price of launching one global public works project, and perhaps a small one at that, the world could escape all the labyrinthine controls, regulations, and social-engineering schemes already being proposed in the name of limiting GHG emissions. (Of course, people who have been relying on climate change as a rationale for reshaping society to conform more closely to their own values and preferences may not account the liberty thus preserved as desirable.)

Naturally, until R&D is completed, geoengineering options remain speculative. The technologies may prove to be ineffectual or to entail intolerable side effects. Geoengineering is also highly "politically incorrect." Nevertheless, the logic behind an exploration of geoengineering is so strong that it is beginning to erode the taboos and prejudices that have hitherto blocked its consideration. The newly elected president of the National Academy of Sciences has become an advocate for exploring various geoengineering concepts, and a growing number of other scientists, including Nobel laureate Dr. Paul Crutzen of the Max Planck Institute, have begun proposing possible approaches. Yet these scientists note the continuing absence of governmental support for these efforts.[53]

In contrast to its neglect of geoengineering, the Bush administration may be overinvesting in other technologies. The poor prospect for GHG controls implies problems for carbon capture and storage. The CCTP's draft strategic plan alludes to the unique vulnerability of CCS to an absence of GHG emission limits. It notes:

While some CCTP-supported advanced technologies may be sufficiently attractive, for a variety of reasons, to find their way into the marketplace at a large scale without supporting policy or incentives, others would not. Even with further technological progress, technologies that capture or sequester CO_2, for example, or others that afford certain climate change-related advantages, are expected to remain more expensive than competing technologies that do not.[54]

This observation highlights a dilemma. The Bush administration has (correctly) disputed claims that China and India will impose mandatory GHG limits. The administration also opposes domestic mandatory emissions limitation policies. But it is emphasizing R&D on technologies that are very unlikely to be deployed without such mandatory limits.

Were total spending higher, such inconsistencies would be less troubling. Some critics of the Bush administration's domestic R&D efforts have called for drastically increased spending, a "new Project Apollo." More realistically, but still ambitiously, one expert has recently proposed that annual spending should amount to at least $5 billion.[55] Although this is a hefty sum that would represent an annual increase of $2 billion in the current CCTP's total budget, advocates of increased spending can certainly point to the large scale of the task of producing multiple technological revolutions.

Nevertheless, such demands are unrealistic. Entitlements and national security needs continue squeezing domestic discretionary spending. The opportunity cost of R&D dollars, moreover, is high; according to John Deutch, "The consensus from studies on the returns to R&D is that the social rates of return are approximately four times higher than the rates of return to other investments."[56] Because society's resources for conducting R&D are limited, increased spending in one area typically involves transferring resources from another. Between 1970 and 1980, roughly half of energy R&D spending occurred at the expense of other R&D programs.[57]

Thus, the CCTP will face tough competition for R&D funds, and the public has a right to expect high returns from dollars allocated to this program. To be able to earn these returns, the CCTP will need a highly cost-effective organizational structure.

CCTP's Organizational Problems

Today, the CCTP is bureaucratically very weak. It has only been appropriated $1 million in fiscal year 2007 to assess, coordinate, and prioritize the program's $3 billion annual expenditures. Management through an interdepartmental committee is problematic from the standpoint of organizational politics, and the Department of Energy already has a competing prioritization system set up around DOE's strategic goals—goals that do not include combating climate change, and, in fact, are at least partially contrary to that purpose. And the federal government also conducts other climate-related technology policies in which CCTP has had little voice.

There are five major organizational problems with the CCTP as it is currently structured. First, many of the CCTP's component efforts are pursuing incremental, near-term agendas. The organizational culture of DOE, its energy industry constituencies, and the legislatively mandated requirements for industry partnerships virtually ensure this temporal myopia. But the short-run focus clashes with the long-run climate policy vision. In the words of the report summarizing the conclusions of the expert review workshops,

> The need to place more emphasis on long-term, revolutionary technologies as well as programs that foster truly innovative, unconventional approaches emerged as essential for meeting the century-long challenge of climate change. This might require a greater percentage of funding to go to potential breakthrough technology versus research that provides only incremental improvements. There is a need for more high-risk but high pay-off research.[58]

Without structural change, the longer-run orientation seems unlikely to receive the optimal attention or funding.

A second problem is that the CCTP's existing components are technology-defined—that is, they are oriented toward advancing specific technologies. That the technologies are very narrowly defined compounds the problem. Climate solutions lying outside of the existing technology stovepipes or cross-cutting them may fall through the cracks. Outside experts have pointed to many examples of promising technologies that appear to suffer from this neglect.[59] To cite just one example, wind turbines deployed in the upper troposphere could, in principle, capture more than enough energy to power global civilization. This energy would be a much more steady power source than surface-level turbines. Successful development of this concept would, in one stride, dramatically improve the odds of successfully coping with climate change and of achieving energy security. DOE's current wind-related R&D, however, is designed to increase the efficiency of turbines operating at low wind speeds, a pervasive challenge for surface-based turbines. DOE labs have therefore declined to fund work on upper-troposphere turbines designed for the consistently high wind speeds that prevail at those altitudes. High-altitude wind turbines may or may not represent an important technological opportunity. Refusing to explore the concept because it does not match existing bureaucratic categories suggests a management problem.

Third, the CCTP has little leverage for keeping spending patterns among its component parts aligned with the pattern that would maximize the effect on climate change. This may seem like a mundane, bureaucratic problem, but it can seriously undermine the effectiveness (and cost-effectiveness) of the program. A recent National Research Council study of the Climate Change Science Program noted the importance of a having a leader "with sufficient authority to allocate resources, direct research effort, and facilitate progress." It also called for a "strategy for setting priorities and allocating resources among different elements of the program (including those that cross agencies) and advancing promising avenues of research."[60] These requirements are equally crucial to the success of CCTP. Yet CCTP does not have the leadership authority, the resources, or the strategic consensus needed to modify spending patterns. Without this, it is hard to say that the program has real leadership.

Fourth, winning approval for enough strategic research (basic scientific research into questions that, if answered, might help solve important social problems) of the right kind will be difficult under the existing organizational structure.[61] Strategic research is essential for CCTP's success.[62] Commendable as the recent cooperation between the CCTP and the Office of Basic Energy Sciences (BES) is, BES should not be the final arbiter of the relative priority of strategic research directed toward climate change versus that directed toward other possible social needs. The current organizational structure subordinates this essentially political-level resource allocation decision to a technical, and only partially accountable, process.

Fifth, the CCTP may lack influence on wider technology policy. The draft strategic plan correctly notes the importance of providing supporting technology policy as a "core approach."[63] So far, we have not seen evidence of success in that endeavor. For instance, the recent energy bill authorized several new subsidies and tax subsidies based in part on their putative climate-related benefits. Obviously, a rational plan would balance the cost-effectiveness of these policies with increased spending within the CCTP. It is doubtful that the CCTP has the resources either to conduct such analysis or to win a serious hearing for its findings.

Conclusion

The Bush administration's domestic climate policy is diverse. It is clearly partly intended as a defensive alternative to domestic cap-and-trade. Given the improbability of successful international GHG controls, domestic emissions limits seem to offer no real prospect of a climate change solution. Both politically and substantively, the president has had reasons for shying away from such proposals.

Despite the real merits of the administration's R&D focus, its policy has not halted the political momentum toward what may eventually become an ineffectual, but potentially fairly expensive, domestic GHG cap-and-trade. This equivocal record of political success suggests the need for a policy reassessment. So far, though, the administration's stance on mandatory controls has remained purely negative.

The administration can lay claim to one vitally important strategic insight: Without new technology, climate policy success would be impossible. Unfortunately, its implementation of this insight has been less than ideal. The focus on mitigation to the exclusion of geoengineering and adaptation is too narrow. Given the spending limitations, the emphasis on carbon capture and storage is probably excessive. Serious organizational problems, some generic, some program-specific, afflict the CCTP. The administration appears oblivious to these problems.

4

A New Climate Policy

Hitherto, the Bush administration has had good political reasons for avoiding the entire subject of climate change. The situation is now altered. Changing circumstances have attenuated many of the previous political barriers to action on climate policy, and the costs of continuing to deemphasize the climate issue have risen.

The Bush administration still has enough time to raise the quality of its climate policy legacy from mediocre to excellent. It cannot do so, however, without seriously rethinking its policy vision. To do that probably requires a new process, with new institutional foundations. Many possible policies might emerge from a new process. This chapter will suggest three possible elements of a new Bush administration climate policy package.

New Political Realities

The Bush administration's earlier reticence toward climate policy in general and mandatory GHG controls in particular was not wrong, but circumstances have changed. Most obviously, the president no longer faces reelection, affording him expanded freedom of political action.

At the same time, the prospect of a new presidential administration taking office in 2009 boosts the urgency of institutionalizing relatively benign mandatory GHG controls, if only to reduce the likelihood of more draconian, misguided measures. If the next president is Senator McCain or a Democrat, he or she would probably enter office already committed to imposition of domestic hard caps. The risk is that the Bush administration will have been only a detour on the road back to Kyoto, rather than the opening of a new, more hopeful climate policy path. Without a greater effort from the current administration, that seems likely.

Some form of mandatory domestic GHG controls is now all but inevitable. Virtually no knowledgeable political observer doubts the truth of this proposition. Despite all the remaining scientific uncertainty, expert warnings about the threat of climate change are rising in volume and pitch. The green pressure groups are entirely committed and immensely well-funded. The visible crumpling of industry resistance to the principle of controls sounds another alarm about the future course of American climate policy. In part, the waning of industry resistance reflects rational calculation of the political odds. The administration would do well to learn from the "political futures market," represented by the way astute private-sector firms are positioning themselves.

In part, some businesses are also trying to use controls as a means of capturing "economic rents"—an term economists use for profits that exceed those needed to hold inputs in their current use. (Noneconomists often use the term "windfall profits" instead of the more anodyne "economic rents.") Under the guise of pursuing some noble-sounding cause, organized interests have often reaped large economic rents by manipulating the legislative process.[1] The fight against harmful climate change is the "plausible pretext" needed to consummate the desired wealth transfers without arousing public indignation.

GHG controls automatically create some opportunities for rent-seeking. For example, controls would boost the costs of fossil-fuel-fired electricity generation. Consequently, wholesale power prices would increase. Nuclear power plants do not emit carbon dioxide, so controls would not increase their costs. GHG controls would, therefore, confer economic rents on the owners of nonemitting (for example, nuclear and renewable) generators. Similarly, the costs of natural-gas-fired power plants would rise less than those of coal-fired plants, creating possible profit opportunities for them as well. Not surprisingly, some power companies with large investments in non-coal-fired facilities have become avid proponents of GHG limits.

The administration should heed the two messages sent by the growing prominence of climate-related rent-seeking. First, this trend reinforces the assessment that mandatory controls are inevitable. Second, it raises a warning flag signaling that controls, when they come, could be needlessly costly and inefficient. Other knowledgeable climate policy commentators are seemingly reaching the same conclusions and also advocating a more active administration response.[2]

Unless the Bush administration wishes to adopt an "*Après moi le déluge*" climate policy, it needs a strategy to preempt the likely results from the interaction of environmentalist ideology and corporate rent-seeking. By shaping the legislation implementing controls, the Bush administration could make GHG limits less costly both now and in the future. The inherent path dependency of government policy places an enormous premium on setting the right precedent. Without a Bush administration initiative, controls are likely to incorporate inefficient command and control and hard cap policies. Either congressionally initiated controls or those proposed by the next president are likely to embody these harmful principles.

A Carbon Tax?

The administration should seriously consider endorsing a modest prophylactic system of economy-wide carbon emissions controls. (By "modest" I mean at a marginal cost of $15 per metric ton of carbon or less.) Such a proposal is not only required to palliate the risks of future economically harmful GHG-control measures; it is also the key to other aspects of a more effective national climate policy.

To be sure, the administration cannot afford another domestic policy defeat like its failure on Social Security. And if the president were to propose a carbon tax (or some other economically less harmful GHG-limitation plan) and fail to get it through Congress, the defeat would harm the future course of American climate policy, not help it. The Bush administration's poor record of legislative success on environmental initiatives suggests that success in this effort would be far from certain. The administration, therefore, would need to conduct a careful political reconnaissance before announcing a new initiative. If the odds were too long, it would probably be best to leave the initiative on the shelf.

At the same time, the potential payoffs from success would be significant and should be weighed carefully against the political costs. Controls could supply government revenue to finance an expanded R&D program. As such, they would enhance the international credibility of America's commitment to increase R&D funding. At the same time, they could lessen, if not end, America's ideological dispute with Europe about mandatory controls, perhaps even enabling the United States to shift the international focus toward R&D funding and away from Kyoto-style cap-and-trade programs.

A Bush administration endorsement of a modest carbon tax would be a very important development in climate change policy. To some observers, this is inconceivable, and would only compound the political unreality of the entire idea of mandatory controls. In their view, President Bush, mindful of his father's experience, would not propose a new tax. Furthermore, the Clinton BTU tax debacle supposedly shows that energy taxes are politically toxic.

This argument, while meriting concern, is also worth challenging, in part because it rests heavily on a self-fulfilling prophecy. The prime reason carbon taxes are politically unrealistic is that "everybody" says they are. Other than that disadvantage, taxes are superior in all respects to the alternatives, and even most of the people who dismiss the feasibility of a tax often concede that substantive superiority. If ever a situation called for political leadership, this is it. True leadership would consist of stating forcefully what virtually everyone knows is true but shuns out of deference to conventional political wisdom.

In fact, contrary to that conventional wisdom, at least some support for the carbon tax already exists. Recently, a very large electric power company and a major environmental think tank jointly endorsed a modest carbon tax.[3] Even without the extra inducement of allowance allocations, some firms would reap economic rents from the imposition of the tax. Many more would back any proposal that promised to remove the threat of more draconian controls. This suggests that a substantial reservoir of potential political support exists, should the administration choose to lead in this direction.

Moreover, careful design can mitigate the alleged political disadvantages of the tax. Most obviously, keeping the tax appropriately modest would minimize its impact on energy prices. Furthermore, many congressional Democrats have endorsed (or voted for) far more costly cap-and-trade programs. These actions hardly position them as credible critics of a carbon tax. By inference, although sniping would be inevitable, the president should not incur serious partisan risk by endorsing a moderate carbon tax. His critics may complain that it is still too little, but they would be in a relatively weak position to stop him.

It must be acknowledged, however, that the choice of a tax would be controversial, particularly within the Republican Party. Again, political intelligence-gathering would have to test the limits of the possible. Certainly, some proponents of mandatory controls would argue that a cap-and-trade might offer some of the advantages of a tax without violating a political taboo. And the right kind of cap-and-trade program would indeed be better than continuing the Bush administration's passive stance on mandatory controls.

Nonetheless, the tax is significantly superior to cap-and-trade. Most critically, a tax avoids all the Kyoto-like problems associated with hard caps. It would be unlikely to encourage emissions cuts that were overly expensive, arbitrary, hasty, or purchased with needless price volatility. It would also be much simpler to administer effectively and, consequently, would be far less costly for both government and the regulated sectors. These advantages imply that a well-structured tax would be far more cost-effective than a cap-and-trade program.

Proponents of cap-and-trade programs argue that a device called a safety valve could minimize the tendency to enact harsh and hasty controls. With an allowance price safety valve, the government offers to sell an unlimited number of allowances at a legislatively determined fixed price, thus setting a ceiling on the price of allowances. Such a provision partially transforms cap-and-trade into a tax. It makes costs more transparent, dampens allowance price fluctuations, and eliminates the risk of needless haste.[4] But this approach merely imitates (incompletely) the advantages of a tax-based approach.

If American controls on GHG must take the form of cap-and-trade, the plan should certainly include a safety valve (and it probably would). Nonetheless, even with the safety valve, cap-and-trade is greatly inferior to a tax. The cumbersome allowance trading system remains an obvious disadvantage. Subtle considerations of political economy may present still worse difficulties.

Perhaps most importantly, the safety valve is relatively weak protection against the later imposition of hard caps in that it lends itself to a political bait-and-switch. By moderating initial costs, the safety valve increases the prospects of enacting a cap-and-trade program. But many cap-and-trade proponents seek to escalate control costs to draconian levels. Once cap-and-trade is in place, these organizations and interests would presumably begin campaigning to eliminate the safety valve—and they would have reasonable prospects for success. The safety valve, by creating large numbers of relatively inexpensive allowances, would effectively nullify any tight quantitative emissions cap. (After all, that is essentially its raison d'être, or at least a necessary effect of its function.) Surely, though, when the safety valve's implication becomes transparent, proponents of hard caps will renew their denunciations of the concept on grounds that the safety valve is subverting the cap. At that point, excising the safety valve would be sufficient to convert relatively cost-effective, price-based controls into an inherently wasteful system of hard caps.

The safety valve also cannot eliminate cap-and-trade's tendency to encourage Congress to squander money on favored special interests. In this regard, a tax is vastly superior. At $10 to $30 per metric ton, carbon controls would generate between $15 billion and $45 billion a year in revenues for the federal government. The president could package the carbon tax as part of a nearly revenue-neutral package. Most carbon tax revenue could be used to fund reductions in economically harmful taxes on capital income. (Lower taxes on capital income would appeal presumably to elements of the business community, and even this mechanism could be used to favor further development and deployment of clean energy facilities.)

Setting aside a relatively small portion of the revenue to fund additional energy R&D would not compromise the logic of this transaction. It would also be consistent with the theme that the president has already sounded on R&D. And experience with transportation taxes suggests that the electorate is much more willing to tolerate tax increases that are linked to specific public spending needs than those aimed at general revenue.

In contrast, cap-and-trade facilitates the diversion of allowances into rent-seeking. A safety valve would only partially ameliorate this problem. Allowances sold under the safety-valve provision would be auctioned and, presumably, the revenue would go to the federal treasury. But there would be little barrier to Congress's natural inclination to give most of the allowances away to favored constituencies. This tendency, if left unchecked, will convert a cap-and-trade system into a revenue loser. About one-third of the value of the allowance stream would be required to offset government revenue losses and price increases caused by the imposition of controls.[5] Precedent indicates, however, that with cap-and-trade, Congress is tempted to distribute most allowances gratis to the affected industries.[6]

In principle, compensation to the industries most severely harmed by the imposition of GHG controls need not convert the controls into a revenue-losing proposition. A perpetual allocation of only about 10 percent of the value of the stream of GHG emissions allowances would fully compensate the fossil-fuel producers and electric power generators for the economic losses occasioned by GHG controls.[7] Thus, capturing large shares of the allowances could turn GHG controls into a source of economic rents for the energy sector, or for some players in it.

Left to its own devices, Congress will enthusiastically consummate this transaction. Cap-and-trade allows the congressional committees of jurisdiction to dole out allowances. With valuable emissions allowances to allocate, members of the relevant committees could confer large financial windfalls on favored (and presumably suitably grateful) interest groups.

A carbon tax, one might correctly object, would offer the tax-writing committees opportunities to confer similar windfalls. However—and this point is key—tax reductions can generate net gains for the economy as a whole, especially if the right taxes are cut.

FIGURE 5
CLIMATE CHANGE GOALS AND POLICY OPTIONS

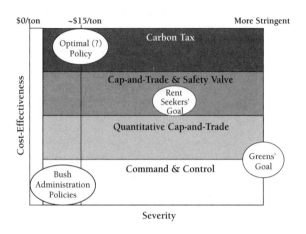

SOURCE: Author's illustration.

All taxes discourage productive activity by reducing individual incentives to invest and to work.[8] Economically, using carbon tax revenues to offset reductions in other taxes would diminish the total macroeconomic costs of the GHG limitations. Politically, tax cuts are popular. Therefore, this kind of carbon tax "revenue recycling" would reduce the costs of GHG controls in a way that also allowed legislators to confer recognizable benefits on their constituents.

In contrast, simply granting emissions allowances to favored companies is merely an income transfer. It creates no corresponding benefit to the larger economy. But congressional committee structure effectively precludes the committees that write cap-and-trade legislation from using emissions allowance sales revenue to fund tax cuts.

Figure 5 sketches some of the relationships between a carbon tax and the goals of other climate policy players.

A New International Negotiation

As already mentioned, one advantage of a domestic mandatory GHG limit would be to place the United States in a strong position to launch a new international negotiation on climate change. Such a negotiation would offer an opportunity to increase international resource commitments directed at minimizing the combined costs of climate change and the countermeasures to it. It could also create a more credible alternative to Kyoto, thus serving an additional defensive purpose.

Climate change is notoriously a global problem. Only international actions can contribute significantly to solutions. (Geoengineering is probably inexpensive enough for a unilateral American solution, but its implications are so pervasive that some degree of global consensus would be required to deploy it.) A common plan of action among major emitters is a prerequisite for success.

For good reasons, the United States does not wish to adopt the Kyoto framework. However, although the administration has created a number of discrete climate change initiatives, it has not proposed a new, superior framework, and it has won fairly few converts to its general approach to the problem. Clearly, the new framework should not be a variant of international cap-and-trade. Other options exist.

There is much to recommend a negotiation designed to create a new international regime on climate change. The regime would presumably coexist with Kyoto, at least initially. For countries feeling trapped in Kyoto, such an agreement might create a broader, more credible, and more accessible escape route than that offered by the Asia-Pacific Partnership. (The APP could, of course, continue to evolve separately.)

One way to create such a regime would be through a so-called bottom-up negotiation. As one observer has noted, "Because differences in national circumstances are so wide any negotiations should allow for different kinds of commitments to be considered."[9] In a bottom-up negotiation, countries would pledge to take certain actions. These might be both international and national, and might cover both mitigation and adaptation. Domestic actions might be of various types:

> For example, industrialized countries would commit to enhanced climate research and to public education and awareness. But especially important would be commitments to technology research and development, so that the technological capacity of these countries would focus on finding solutions to the longer-term issues and needs of sustainable economic and social development.[10]

Offers could also include adoption of hard targets or specific emissions control policies. Countries would offer analysis linking actions to results with regard to mitigating, offsetting, or adapting to climate change.[11]

In such a negotiation, the United States might pursue several objectives. Most important would be to seek R&D cost-sharing agreements with other countries. Making an increase in national R&D spending contingent on a comparable contribution from others increases the investment's potential benefits. Such agreements, therefore, could increase the total pool of R&D funds.[12] Much the same logic would apply to research on climate science.

With respect to technology diffusion, the same kinds of market distortions at work in India and China operate in many other developing countries. It might be possible to engage other large developing economies in the task of correcting the distortions that increase their GHG-intensity. Christopher Green has suggested the possibility of seeking an international agreement on the protection of intellectual property that is demonstrably linked to climate solutions.[13] The U.N. Framework Convention on Climate Change could become the forum for a bottom-up negotiation on climate. But the UNFCCC is only one option. The UNFCCC involves many countries with little influence on climate change. And it is dominated by environmental ministries that are often ideologically driven. One commentator recently observed that the UNFCCC involves "too many countries, too few ministries." If the EU counts for one, twenty or so countries account for the vast preponderance of the world's GHG emissions. There is no reason for not initiating a negotiation among them. Two possible forums for these discussions are an expanded G8 or a slightly expanded International Energy Agency.

In the past, negotiations focused on burden-sharing have dealt successfully with complex problems. NATO and the Marshall Plan are two salient examples.[14] Such negotiations are not necessarily easy; they involve weighing of disparate contributions and consideration of different national circumstances. But at least they avoid requiring commitments to achieve specific results in the face of great uncertainty about prospective costs and benefits.

Bottom-up negotiations would allow nations to leverage their own commitments by bargaining for reciprocity, thus moving the system closer to an efficient cooperative level of effort. Unlike top-down negotiations limited to bargaining solely about short-run emissions cuts, a bottom-up negotiation would escape the strait-jacket of requiring differently situated countries to offer only a single type of effort. An international bazaar that can accept many kinds of currency—or barter—is likely to do more business than one restricted to a single (restrictive) medium of exchange.

This aspect of bottom-up negotiation would enhance the prospects for successful climate policy. Short-run OECD emissions reductions, as discussed above, are environmentally insignificant. And GHG cuts from China and India, as already noted, will likely prove more elusive than is generally assumed. Thus, better-funded or better-organized R&D—an outcome that might emerge from a bottom-up negotiation—could contribute more to the long-term solution to climate change than would another round of costly, environmentally insignificant, short-run emissions cuts.

The concept of a bottom-up negotiation also offers political advantage to the Bush administration. The need for Republican unity in the Senate was an important determinant of early Bush administration climate policy. Now, however, several Republican senators, especially members of the Foreign Relations Committee, express concern about what they perceive as American diplomatic isolation. A bottom-up negotiation could alleviate these concerns.

Without active support from the United States, a bottom-up negotiation on climate is impossible. Just as the United States played the leadership role in the NATO and Marshall Plan negotiations, it must lead if meaningful negotiations on climate are to occur. Other countries are likely to be responsive. Japan's METI, for example, has shown some interest in the concept of a bottom-up negotiation on climate.[15] Perhaps Canada's new government, which seems to be in closer touch with climate policy reality than was its predecessor, might wish to initiate talks; certainly, it is likely at least to be a constructive partner in them. Ultimately, though, the United States must play a lead role.

Building Better R&D Institutions and Policies

Proposals for either domestic emissions limits or a new, bottom-up international negotiation would represent considerable innovations in climate policy. The Bush administration does not, however, need to restart its climate policy from scratch. The R&D component of the existing policy is sound. The administration mainly needs to restructure the program's research agenda and organizational structure so as to increase the prospects of success.

How to organize publicly funded climate-related R&D is one of the most crucial questions of climate policy.[16] Solutions must attack the continuing problem of DOE's organizational structure. The creation of an independent R&D agency within DOE to conduct this research, a so-called ARPA-E (Advanced Research Projects Agency-Energy), is a promising potential solution. The proposal to create ARPA-E is modeled after the Defense Advanced Research Projects Agency (DARPA).

The ARPA-E concept would have several key features. It would aim for large-scale, high-risk transformative technological advances. It would emphasize "outside-the-box" thinking and innovative approaches. It would operate with a small staff and would commission research, not conduct it. It would have great freedom to contract with the best-qualified research entities. Personnel would be recruited for relatively short five- to ten-year tenures. The agency would have great discretion to initiate and terminate projects.

ARPA-E would foster strategic (Pasteur's Quadrant) research—basic science that is directly relevant to solving urgent practical problems in the energy system. It would also fund more advanced and perhaps proof-of-concept technology development. It would not fund technology deployment. It would make use of inducement prizes and other innovative incentives to encourage targeted R&D.

This model has been spectacularly successful in the Department of Defense. DARPA has produced a long string of revolutionary new technologies and inspired breakthroughs that have benefited both the military and civilian sides of the American economy enormously. It has fostered crucially important advances in human/computer interface, the internet, global positioning satellites, precision strike weapons, stealth technology, drones, intelligence satellites, and many other technologies.[17] Recently, an expert with long DOE experience (and a former director of DARPA) summarized DOE's structural problem. He went on to propose a solution: an agency structured like DARPA. DOE, he wrote,

> has too many disparate missions to be managed effectively as a coherent organization. . . . Because of all this multi-layered cross cutting, there is no one accountable for the operation of any part of the organization but the Secretary, and no Secretary has the time to lead the whole thing effectively. By setting up a semi-autonomous agency, many of these problems go away. If the agency screws up, the agency director is directly accountable and if heads must roll, his/hers is the head. An important benefit is the semi-autonomous agency could clearly recruit top talent, since leading such an agency would be among the best technical management jobs in the nation. DARPA, NOAA and the NSA are successful organizations that fit this mold.[18]

Accepting similar logic, a recent National Academy of Sciences panel proposed creating ARPA-E.[19] Bills were introduced in both

House and Senate to implement this recommendation, the Senate bill having over sixty cosponsors.

Despite these strong recommendations, some observers question whether ARPA-E can succeed. They have argued that government simply cannot do effective R&D, and that energy technologies, unlike defense technologies, must be sold to the private sector, a task at which a DARPA-like entity would fail. Extending this argument, some skeptics claim that the private sector is more cost-sensitive than the military market, and some worry that private-sector product design is a more multifaceted challenge than defense-sector product design.

Each of these arguments, however, is based, at best, on a half-truth, and some do not even meet that standard. First, the success of DARPA answers the crudely ideological objection that government R&D cannot succeed. It demonstrates, moreover, that success can be sustained over time. DARPA has been operating successfully since the 1950s, and the performance of the National Institutes of Health (NIH) shows that it is not an isolated case. That some government R&D has been unsuccessful is doubtless true, but the overall history disproves the proposition that government R&D is somehow inherently inefficient.

Second, history also shows that many DARPA-developed technologies have successfully penetrated the private market. Examples include DARPA-inspired innovations in computer science, the internet, global positioning satellites, and materials science. DARPA led the way in the successful resuscitation of the American semiconductor industry, while NIH-sponsored innovations have had similarly pervasive effects in health care. If new government-fostered technologies offer economic payoffs, the private sector will adopt them, even if the civilian applications are motivated by concerns quite distant from those of government.

Third, government has many means of encouraging private-sector adoption of technologies it favors. The private sector may, in fact, be more cost-sensitive than the military. But government can use taxes, regulations, and subsidies to change the relative costs of technologies it wishes to promote. In any case, industries facing economy-wide regulations or incentives might actually be less cost-sensitive than armed services competing for limited budget authorities.

Fourth, private-sector innovation does not necessarily present problems more multidimensional than those confronting DARPA. For example, relatively simple commodity markets are common in the energy sector, although prices are famously volatile. It is far from evident that such markets pose more complex problems than, say, the Soviet threat to Western Europe during the 1980s. Cartel theory is straightforward compared to the complexities introduced by the myriad possible enemy countermeasures that might be deployed to thwart a defense technology.

The real threat to the effectiveness of ARPA-E is not differences in the market for defense and energy technologies. It is in the political differences between making defense policy and energy policy. Congress tends to pervert R&D into pork barrel politics.[20] In the case of DARPA, political forces restrained this tendency, likely because the opportunities for defense pork are so large that DARPA could "fly under the radar"—there are too many richer targets in the defense budget. And the secretary of defense's considerable bargaining power may have protected the agency.

It is not certain that DOE's different circumstances and institutional environment would similarly protect ARPA-E. Without strong support from the Department of Defense's upper management, DARPA could not have succeeded.[21] A fledgling ARPA-E, if placed in DOE, will certainly fail without strong backing from the secretary of energy. The administration's initial resistance to the concept bodes ill for its willingness to faithfully implement it.

The Bush administration should, therefore, endorse the ARPA-E concept and ensure that the energy secretary is committed to making it work. Creating ARPA-E is not enough. The new agency will fail unless it is nurtured and held to high standards. Doing so has to be part of the secretary's job.

ARPA-E may not live up to DARPA's illustrious record. Nevertheless, it should be an improvement over DOE's existing incremental stovepiped technology programs, operating under business-as-usual methods.

ARPA-E is the single most important reform of energy-related R&D. Several other options, however, might improve on the rather disappointing status quo as well. For starters, the structure of the administration's Climate Change Technology Program should be reconsidered. Applying the National Research Council's findings about the Climate Change Science Program to the CCTP suggests that the ability to redistribute resources among the program's components is one key to success. The simplest solution would be for the CCTP to have a budget of its own. Currently, the program lacks the resources to conduct even minimal planning and coordination functions. Without a more adequate resource-base of money and personnel, it can accomplish nothing.

But more would be needed to make the CCTP effective. The CCTP should have the resources to buy research and development from other entities, public and private, subject to a merit review process. (If an organization based in DOE's policy shop cannot, for political reasons, have a significant budget, the CCTP should be bureaucratically relocated to become part of ARPA-E.)

With a research budget, the CCTP would be transformed from an unwelcome and ineffectual nag into a desired customer and potential source of funds. The various R&D providers within government and beyond it would compete for these funds. Gone would be the bureaucratic multi-agency committee trying to override the centrifugal forces and misaligned incentives of the research suppliers. This approach would create a quasi-market within government and beyond it. It would encourage CCTP's current component programs to behave more consistently with the larger goals of climate policy. Where resource shortages hindered performance, CCTP would be able to help.

The CCTP should also have authority to spend its discretionary funds on exploratory research and strategic (or Pasteur's Quadrant)[22] research related to climate. The CCTP's draft strategic plan proposes such expenditures.[23] Actually implementing the exploratory research program proposed in the plan would compensate for the CCTP's currently rigid stovepiped organization. The program could allocate funds from a small discretionary account among its constituent parts, enabling it to seek out innovative solutions wherever they might exist. A small amount of seed money would be available to develop promising technologies. The CCTP would hand off to larger programs those technologies that successfully withstood initial scrutiny.

The CCTP should also be authorized to use its budget for "strategic research," and it should acquire the research it wants from whom it wishes.[24] This arrangement would provide clearer accountability than does the current situation, in which the Office of Basic Energy Sciences determines what strategic research to fund with little in the way of clear performance standards.

If an ARPA-E were created within DOE, the CCTP's functions could be folded into it. If it were created outside of DOE, it should take over climate-related exploratory and strategic research. In that case, the CCTP should continue to exist within DOE. It should have a budget in order to readjust spending within the existing technology stovepipes and encourage a focus on R&D related to climate change.

In addition to creating an ARPA-E and reforming the CCTP, there are other steps that the administration could take to boost the effectiveness of American climate-related R&D:

- The CCTP's activities should be expanded to include exploration of geoengineering. An ARPA-E is the logical entity to do this exploration.

- For reasons already discussed, the APP should be organized around the strategy of encouraging targeted economic reforms in India and China.

- The United States should encourage other nations to adopt climate-related R&D strategic plans. More transparency is likely to highlight both duplication and institutional deficiencies and would generally increase the efficiency of the various national R&D programs.

- The CCTP should be empowered to use inducement prizes, as DARPA and NASA are authorized to do.[25] Congress is ambivalent about prizes. Although it has authorized some limited prize competitions, it often resists them as limiting the ability of congressional committees to use R&D as political pork. The DOE bureaucracy may also find prizes threatening to existing funding and to comfortable business patterns. These objections underscore the virtues of the prize concept.

Beyond these structural issues, the administration's climate-related technology policy cries out for a serious strategic assessment. The previous chapter questioned the CCTP's policy of excluding work on geoengineering and adaptation. For several reasons, the existing policy seems wrong on its face.

First, the administration now publicly states that climate change is potentially serious. It also argues that Kyoto will not halt it, and it has not proposed any abatement initiatives remotely large enough to have a significant impact. In fact, such options may not be available. The need to determine the feasibility of geoengineering seems like an unavoidable inference. (The need for R&D on adaptation should be equally obvious.)

Second, confirmation of geoengineering's feasibility should change other R&D priorities. Even if geoengineering were to prove imperfect, confidence that mankind can avert catastrophic climate change would allow a much longer-term approach to developing mitigation technologies. More time would reduce costs and avoid the stampede to unappealing options like expensive carbon capture and storage or converting the transportation energy system to hydrogen.

Third, confirmation of geoengineering's cost-effectiveness would obviate the appeal of expensive mitigation strategies motivated by the fear of speculative low-probability results. Geoengineering would provide the scram button that would allow the global energy system to run longer, harder, and more cheaply than would be prudent without this fallback strategy. There is an intriguing possibility that geoengineering would yield net benefits regardless of climate change. These non–climate-related benefits might be substantial in comparison with the costs of implementing albedo modification. As

Edward Teller and his colleagues have observed, the costs of albedo modification

> appear to be an order-of-magnitude less than health-care savings in the U.S. alone due to avoidance of UV skin damage—and far less than increased agricultural productivity due to avoidance of crop photodamage in the U.S. alone; thus, the cost to the U.S. taxpayer of implementing this system of benefit to all humanity . . . would appear to be quite negative: its direct economic benefits of several dozen billion dollars annually would greatly outweigh its $1–2 B/year costs (corresponding to counteracting CO_2 levels 2–4 times those of pre-industrial times).[26]

Finally, if new evidence suggested that geoengineering would not work or would produce unacceptable side effects, the case for mitigation would become less ambiguous. Experiments and modeling to test geoengineering might also produce new insights into climate science. Today, climate-modeling suggests that some forms of geo-engineering are likely to work. Falsifying that hypothesis would almost certainly produce new understanding.

Institutional and Intellectual Foundations for a New Climate Policy

The Bush administration clearly has a unified climate policy vision, but it is too narrow and too shallow. It cannot either solve the climate problem or successfully deflate demand for harmful and ineffective climate policy patent medicines. The Bush administration needs a climate policy that is both intellectually stronger and more fully explained to the policy community and the public.

Many criticized the CCTP strategic plan because it covered only technology. These complaints seem misplaced. Developing a technology plan is a valid and important exercise in its own right. In a larger sense, though, the critics have a point: The administration has never clearly enunciated the larger policy vision into which the CCTP plan would fit.

The relative weakness of the policy analysis (and public education) on climate policy raises an institutional question. Is the administration properly organized to manage this issue? Some commentators have charged that the Bush administration's centralized management encourages superficial, overly politicized analysis.[27]

Whatever the general merits of this assertion, it seems to apply at least in part to climate policy. If a new policy is, in fact, needed, the administration also needs a much stronger institutional framework to forge it and oversee its implementation. The Bush administration has yet to meld its several valid insights into a coherent vision and to support that vision with an effective action plan.

One way of doing so would be to establish a presidential commission. This is a common tool for executive branch efforts to explore options, conduct needed policy analysis, float trial balloons, and build national consensus. A commission would also be a means of giving the president "new reasons" for boosting the priority of climate change and reversing his position on the need for mandatory controls. Because no American climate policy can be credible without these steps, commission recommendations could provide political "cover" for the course change. Naturally, the composition of the commission and its influence on the policymaking process are crucial variables that would ultimately determine its effectiveness.

A cabinet-level study committee might be another means of achieving the same objective. Placing the vice president in charge of the committee would have important political advantages. In particular, because Vice President Dick Cheney has a reputation as a skeptic on climate change, he is uniquely well-positioned to make the case that such a course correction is unavoidable. As someone knowledgeable about the energy sector, Cheney would also presumably resist the seductive allure of mistaking symbols for reality, an intellectual sin common in the discussion of mandatory GHG limits. This approach could be effective—if the vice president were to embrace the goal of developing a new, more robust climate policy. But the vice president and the entire cabinet were intimately involved in the administration's review of climate policy in 2001–2; it is not clear whether revisiting the issue now would produce different results.

Whichever institutional vehicle is selected, it should take up an aggressive agenda of policy analysis. The Bush administration has so far done a mediocre job of critiquing Kyoto-style cap-and-trade, and a worse job of enunciating alternatives to it. The administration needs to use policy analysis to build a sound intellectual foundation for rational climate policy. This process should involve establishing a policy research agenda, doing the analysis needed to answer its central questions, and presenting a fully documented case for those answers.

To date, even when climate policy questions have been under review by the administration, scant effort has been devoted to providing the sort of robust policy analysis that might influence the public debate. It would not be an exaggeration to say that there simply has not been any systematic climate change policy research in this administration. In fact, the White House has not allocated the resources that would be required to do such research and analysis. The White House has only had one or at most two analysts devoted to climate policy, a resource commitment far below that of the Clinton administration. The executive branch has also made few efforts to raise the level of the national and international climate policy debate. Where it has intervened, as with the early request to the National Academy of Sciences, the effort was focused on narrowly scientific questions, and the follow-up on the policy implications of those findings was half-hearted.

In the American governmental system, the executive branch holds a dominant position as a supplier of sophisticated policy analysis. It is the best-positioned branch of government to surmount particularistic and demagogic pressures. Hence, the Bush administration's abdication of climate policy leadership has contributed to the paucity of rigorous economic analysis. While European governments continue churning out pro-Kyoto propaganda, the American executive branch has subsided into analytic silence. Whether this silence reflects overconfidence, the issue's low priority, or pure anti-intellectualism is hard to assess; it may be some combination of all three factors.

Certainly, the administration has not pursued an active research agenda on climate policy. Important questions are unanswered— indeed, unaddressed. A few examples may suffice to suggest the need:

- Although the Energy Policy Act's Title XVI suggests a policy of targeted market reforms in the developing world, specific implementation of this strategy requires detailed analysis. Questions extend to the distorting policies that might be targeted, the factors that encourage their preservation, and the leverage for reform. The administration is not undertaking this analysis in a comprehensive way, although integrating findings from various bilateral and multilateral international dialogues and working groups would be a start.

- Much current speculation about technological solutions to climate change depends heavily on optimistic assumptions about learning by doing. A more nuanced assessment is likely to refine these assumptions significantly and produce more realistic expectations.[28] There is an important need to assess the implications of the economic literature on this subject and how they might apply to the technologies now being developed and subsidized.

- In general, the economic implications of climate change are less well-studied than the science. The Intergovernmental Panel on Climate Change (IPCC) analyses of climate change economics may be somewhat alarmist. The recent report by the Economics Committee of the British House of Lords raised several examples of possible instances of this bias, each of which might be examined more carefully.[29]

- Many economists criticize the arbitrariness with which Kyoto and its domestic analogues have set emissions-reduction targets. The Bush administration has echoed this criticism. Yet the administration has never proposed a superior alternative. Intensity targets (even putting aside the fact that the administration's targets are voluntary and, hence, largely meaningless) merely substitute a different kind of arbitrary standard for Kyoto's arbitrary hard caps. A rational policy would set a price for carbon emissions based on expected damages from emissions. Failure to propose an economically rational standard leaves the Kyoto process as the only game in town.

- Among experts, there is considerable debate over R&D strategy. Broadly, some recommend a technologically ambitious strategy aimed at achieving multiple, large-scale technological breakthroughs. Others suggest concentration on shorter-term, more incremental progress. Despite the central role played by R&D in its climate strategy, the Bush administration has undertaken no systematic assessment of these rival strategies.

Economists and political scientists could probably easily expand this list. The main point is clear, however: The Bush administration has not bothered to generate a policy research agenda related to climate change.

Conclusion

Much of the criticism of the administration's climate policy is wrong. Most environmental advocates believe the president erred in rejecting Kyoto or in not proposing a more acceptable version of cap-and-trade. That is not my opinion.

In fact, for the foreseeable future, international GHG controls cannot noticeably diminish GHG emissions. The president is right to eschew commitments to such policies. If his opposition is to be politically successful, though, the administration must develop an alternative policy that offers a realistic prospect of ameliorating the potential harm from climate change. Only a policy that offers a more effective counter to the threat of climate change will provide a credible alternative to the ineffectual and economically harmful model represented by the Kyoto Protocol and analogous proposals for domestic hard caps.

The Bush administration has endorsed strategies that, if implemented successfully, might eventually diminish the potential harm from climate change. Specifically, R&D might someday greatly reduce the costs of abating GHG emissions. Dramatically lower abatement costs could decrease the odds against implementing effective international GHG controls. Alternatively, geoengineering technologies could eliminate the need to reduce GHG emissions or push it far into the future.

An R&D-centered climate policy is admittedly a gamble. Even with the best possible R&D program, no one can guarantee that the right technologies will materialize. If they did materialize, lower abatement costs and higher net benefits of abatement might still prove insufficient to defeat international free-riding. The justification for betting on R&D is that, without better technologies, the future is likely to hold both very high abatement costs and high risks from climate change.

In light of the difficulty of the challenge, the Bush administration needs a stronger and better-articulated climate policy. It is far from certain that it will adopt a course correction in this area. Nevertheless, an engaged conservative administration could contribute a valuable corrective to the quixotic climate solutions of the left. Such a conservative agenda could include four elements:

- A small carbon tax could complement the R&D strategy. It would simultaneously offer benign symbolism and much-needed federal revenue. It would make Bush administration climate policy more credible without imposing excessive costs. While a carbon tax may be politically impracticable, its potential advantages are so great that the administration should conduct a serious political reconnaissance to determine whether proposing a tax (or even a cap-and-trade program with a safety valve) would represent politically viable proposals.

- If the administration were to embrace mandatory GHG controls it could then also initiate a bottom-up international negotiation on climate policy. (A negotiation without the prospect of controls might be possible but would be less promising.) The negotiation should seek to obtain a variety of reciprocal national commitments aimed at combating climate change and diminishing its potentially harmful consequences. Its principlal goal would be increased R&D directed at developing high-potential climate-related technologies. Ideally, the negotiation would be conducted outside of the UNFCCC framework.

- With or without a carbon tax, the administration should restructure the current federal R&D effort. Addressing the organizational problems with DOE's R&D efforts is vital. The best solution would be to create an Advanced Research Projects Agency within DOE. The climate-related R&D portfolio should be expanded to encompass work on geoengineering and adaptation. Increased funding for climate-related R&D is probably justified, but only if DOE has first corrected existing problems with its research agenda and organizational structure.

- The administration should build an institutional foundation for analyzing and implementing an innovative climate policy. It might use a presidential commission or cabinet-level task force for this purpose. The administration needs to implement an aggressive agenda of policy research and analysis. Ultimately, the administration should establish the precedent of formulating a comprehensive climate strategy encompassing science, technology, diplomacy, and domestic policy.

Paradoxically, an effective conservative approach to climate change could, in fact, turn out to be one of George W. Bush's most important policy achievements, if the administration makes it a priority in its final two years in office.

Notes

Introduction

1. Ermarth (1978), 316.
2. North (1990), 3–4.
3. In North's terminology, which this book adopts, "institutions" refers to rules, formal and informal. The practices used in enforcing rules are also institutions. "Organizations" are groups that function within various institutional arrangements. Thus, the rules of football and the ways in which the officials apply them are institutions. Teams and leagues are organizations.

Chapter 1: The Bush Administration and the Kyoto Protocol

1. Samuelson (2006).
2. Odom and Dujarric (2004), 45.
3. Mandelbaum (2005), 6–11.
4. Odom and Dujarric (2004), 56.
5. Lal (1999), 42–43.
6. This assumed Annex I emission rights trading.
7. Hourcade and Shukla (2001), table 8.8, 537.
8. Nordhaus and Boyer (2000), 154.
9. Ibid., 152.
10. Parts of this book rely rather heavily on the Nordhaus-Boyer analysis (2000). In my view, the Nordhaus-Boyer work remains the best available. However, the analysis is now six years old. A later section of the book speculates on how later findings might modify the Nordhaus-Boyer estimates. It also explains why, in my opinion, the net effect of these modifications is likely to be small. See Nordhaus and Boyer (2000), table 8-7, 160.

11. Ibid., table 7-3, 130.

12. Ibid., 161.

13. Ibid.

14. Albrecht-Carrie (1958), 442.

15. Barrett (2003), 384.

16. Based on United Nations Framework Convention on Climate Change (2005), table 5.

17. Environmental News Service (2006).

18. Hennessy (2005), A13.

19. Nordhaus and Boyer (2000), table 7-3, 130.

20. Commission of the European Communities (2005), 3.

21. Smith (2006).

22. Nordhaus (2005), 15.

23. Pizer (1999), 1.

24. Hennessy (2005), A13.

25. Lucas (2005).

26. Blair (2005).

27. The resolution of the scientific controversy about hurricanes and climate change remains in doubt. However, claiming that a reversal of the U.S. stance on Kyoto would have affected ocean temperatures in the Gulf of Mexico in the year 2005 is preposterous.

28. Szabo (2004), 137.

29. Ibid., 147.

30. Thorning (2002), 1.

31. North (1990), 99.

32. U.S. Senate (2006a), 3.

33. Ibid., 5.

34. Ibid.

35. Bodman (2006), 3.

36. U.S. Senate (2006b), 3.

37. Ibid., 5–6.

38. Ibid., 6.

39. Ibid., 7.

40. U.S. Department of State (2006), 4.

41. Dobriansky (2005), 5–6.

42. Barrett (2004), 13.

43. Ibid., 14.

44. U.S. House of Representatives (2006a).

45. The president's father's administration announced a "no regrets" climate policy, meaning that it emphasized measures that reduced GHG

emissions while achieving other laudable goals unrelated to climate change.

Chapter 2: The Chimera of Global GHG Cap-and-Trade

1. Chang, Mendelsohn, and Shaw (2003), 5–6.
2. Nordhaus and Boyer (2000), table 7-6.
3. Ibid., table 7-7.
4. Ibid., table 7-3.
5. Popp (2004), 4–5.
6. Hoffert et al. (2002), 981.
7. Edmonds and Stokes (2003), 163.
8. Nordhaus (2001), 284.
9. Popp (2004), 15.
10. Montgomery and Smith (2005), 20.
11. Nordhaus (2005), 7–8.
12. Prinn (2004), 301.
13. Jacoby (2004), 309.
14. Schelling (2005), 582.
15. Arnold (1990), 24.
16. North (1990), 28.
17. Barrett (2004), 10.
18. Nordhaus and Yang (1996), 762.
19. Ibid., 753.
20. Barrett (2003), 270.
21. Schelling (2005), 588.
22. Nordhaus (2005), 17.
23. Ibid., 17.
24. Leopold (2004), 2.
25. Schelling (2005), 588.
26. Ibid.
27. Barrett (2003), 379.
28. Stavins (1996), 298.
29. Japan. Ministry of Economy, Trade and Industry (2004), 27.
30. Yang and Jacoby (1997), 4.
31. "Leakage" is a term used to describe the migration of GHG-intensive activities and industries from jurisdictions with stringent controls to jurisdictions without controls or with less stringent limits. Leakage imposes economic costs but changes only the geographic pattern of emissions. The emissions persist.

32. Schelling (2002), 3.
33. Aldy (2004), 107–8.
34. Stavins (1996), 298.
35. Nordhaus and Yang (1996), 756–57.
36. Wirl, Huber, and Walker (1998), 218.
37. Grundig, Ward, and Zorick (2001), 155.
38. Cooper (2004), 7–8.
39. Dam (2006), 15–20.
40. Montgomery and Tuladhar (2006, draft), 54.
41. Heller and Shukla (2003), 118.
42. Ibid., 126.
43. "Anyway tons," as the term implies, are emission "reductions" that will occur without a policy change because, for various reasons, the baseline of emissions growth is often exaggerated.
44. Barrett (2003), 379.

Chapter 3: Bush Administration Domestic Climate Policy

1. Pizer (2004), 15.
2. Ibid., 38.
3. Barnes (2006), 22–23.
4. Homer-Dixon (2002), 498.
5. Kempton, Boster, and Hartley (1999), 141–43, 85.
6. Ladd and Bowman (1995), 32.
7. Gallup Organization (2006a), 6–10.
8. Ibid., 10.
9. Nivola and Crandall (1995), 110–11.
10. Jones (2001), 101.
11. Gallup Organization (2006a) 4, 5.
12. Ibid., 8.
13. Kingdon (1995), 184.
14. Barnes (2006), 20.
15. Ladd and Bowman (1995), 44–45.
16. Gallup Organization (2006b), 191.
17. Ibid., 323.
18. Hunton and Williams (2006).
19. Keeler (2004), 2.
20. Fichthorn and Wood (2005), 2–4.
21. U.S. Senate (2005), 1.
22. Bush (2001), 3.

23. Ibid., 2.
24. Prinn (2004), 299, 300.
25. Jacoby (2004), 308.
26. Bush (2001), 3.
27. Pizer (2004), 37.
28. David Conover, in conversation with the author, May 13, 2006.
29. Pizer (2004), 37.
30. Dinan and Austin (2003).
31. O'Keefe (2006), 2.
32. Nivola and Crandall (1995), 94.
33. Pizer (2004), 13.
34. Aldy (2004), 110.
35. Deutch (2005), 3.
36. Ibid., 5.
37. Caldeira et al. (2005), 4–6.
38. Aldy (2004), 101.
39. North (1990), 94.
40. Green et al. (2005), 6.
41. O'Keefe and Kueter (2006), 18–19.
42. U.S. Climate Change Technology Program (2005), 2-2n2.
43. Brown et al. (2006), xi.
44. Smith (2004), 31.
45. Cooper (1999), 43.
46. Nordhaus and Boyer (2000), 98.
47. A "scram" is the rapid emergency shutdown of a nuclear reactor or other system.
48. Keith and Dowlatabadi (1992), 293.
49. Hoffert et al. (2002), 986.
50. Teller et al. (2004), 5–6.
51. Schelling (2005), 592.
52. National Academy of Sciences (1992), 460.
53. Broad (2006), 1–4.
54. U.S. Climate Change Technology Program (2005), 2-11.
55. Deutch (2005), 8.
56. Popp (2004), 17.
57. Ibid.
58. Brown et al. (2006), xi.
59. Caldeira et al. (2005), 4–6.
60. National Research Council (2005), 80.
61. Dr. John Marburger, following the terminology of the late Donald

Stokes, refers to research in Pasteur's Quadrant in a way that seems to correspond closely with the concept of "strategic research"; Marburger (2005), 1.

62. U.S. Climate Change Technology Program (2005), 9-6–9-7.

63. Ibid., 2-10–2-11.

Chapter 4: A New Climate Policy

1. Pareto (1966), 115.

2. Saunders and Turekian (2006), 81.

3. Hanson and Hendricks (2006).

4. Hubbard and Stiglitz (2003), 2.

5. Smith, Ross, and Montgomery (2002), figure 1, 16.

6. Joskow and Schmalensee (1997).

7. At this percentage of allowances the energy sector as a whole would break even, although some individual firms would still incur losses. A larger share of the total allowance stream (not calculated in the cited study, but very likely less than half) would be required to eliminate all losses to all individual firms. Because controls would confer economic rents on some firms, and financial gains and losses would be unevenly distributed, some firms could still lose although the sector was breaking even. See Smith, Ross, and Montgomery (2002), 25.

8. Ibid., 4.

9. Reinstein (2004), 3.1.

10. Ibid., 3.3.

11. Ibid.

12. Barrett (2004), 13.

13. Christopher Green, personal correspondence with the author, May 23, 2006.

14. Schelling (2005), 589.

15. Japan. Ministry of Economy, Trade and Industry (2004), 18.

16. Montgomery and Smith (2005), 39.

17. U.S. House of Representatives (2006b), 13–16.

18. Reis (1999), 4.

19. National Academy of Sciences (2006), 6–15.

20. Cohen and Noll (1991), 2–3.

21. van Atta (2005), 6.

22. The late Donald Stokes argued for greater government emphasis on questions that raised fundamental scientific issues that also had high potential for social betterment. He designated questions that met these

conditions as falling within what he termed "Pasteur's Quadrant." Stokes (1997).

23. U.S. Climate Change Technology Program (2005), 2-7, 9-1.

24. Ibid.

25. Newell and Wilson (2005), 4.

26. Teller et al. (2004), 5.

27. Bartlett (2006), 26.

28. Nordhaus (2004), 28.

29. United Kingdom. Parliament. House of Lords (2005), 58.

References

Albrecht-Carrie, Rene. 1958. *A Diplomatic History of Europe Since the Congress of Vienna*. New York: Harper.

Aldy, Joseph A. 2004. Saving the Planet Cost-Effectively: The Role of Economic Analysis in Climate Change Mitigation Policy. In *Painting the White House Green: Rationalizing Environmental Policy Inside the Executive Office of the President*, ed. Randall Lutter and Jason F. Shogren. Washington, D.C.: Resources for the Future.

Arnold, R. Douglas. 1990. *The Logic of Congressional Action*. New Haven: Yale University Press.

Barnes, Fred. 2006. *Rebel-in-Chief: Inside the Bold and Controversial Presidency of George W. Bush*. New York: Crown Forum.

Barrett, Scott. 2003. *Environment & Statecraft: The Strategy of Environmental Treaty-Making*. New York: Oxford University Press.

———. 2004. Kyoto Plus. In *Climate Change Policy*, ed. D. Helm. Oxford: Oxford University Press.

Bartlett, Bruce. 2006. *Imposter: How George W. Bush Bankrupted America and Betrayed the Reagan Legacy*. New York: Doubleday.

Blair, Tony. 2005. Oral Answers to Questions—Prime Minister: Engagements. *Parliamentary Debates*. Commons. Session 2005-06, col. 965, November 16. Available at: http://www.publications.parliament.uk/pa/cm200506/cmhansrd/cm051116/debtext/51116-03.htm#column_960 (last accessed October 8, 2006).

Bodman, Samuel (U.S. energy secretary). 2006. Asia-Pacific Partnership Ministerial Statement. Remarks before the Asia-Pacific Partnership (APP) Ministerial Conference on Clean Development and Climate, Sydney, Australia. January 12.

Broad, William D. 2006. How to Cool the Planet (Maybe). *New York Times*, June 27.

Brown, Marilyn A., Matt Antes, Charlotte Franchuk, Burton H. Koske, Gordon Michaels, and Joan Pellegrino. 2006. Results of a Technical

Review of the U.S. Climate Change Technology Program's R&D Portfolio. Oak Ridge National Laboratory, Oak Ridge, Tenn., May.

Bush, George W. 2001. Remarks by President Bush on Global Climate Change. White House Rose Garden, Washington, D.C., June 11, http://www.state.gov/g/oes/rls/rm/4149.htm (accessed October 4, 2006).

Caldeira, Kenneth, Danny Day, William Fulkerson, and Lee Lane. 2005. Climate Change Technology Exploratory Research (CCTER). Climate Policy Center, Washington, D.C., December.

Chang, Ching-Cheng, Robert Mendelsohn, and Daigee Shaw. 2003. *Global Warming and the Asian Pacific*. Northampton, Mass.: Edward Elgar Publishing, Inc.

Cohen, Linda R., and Roger G. Noll. 1991. *The Technology Pork Barrel*. Washington, D.C.: Brookings Institution Press

Commission of the European Communities. 2005. Winning the Battle Against Global Climate Change. Communication from the Commission to the Council, the European Parliament, the European Economic and Social Committee, and the Committee of the Regions, Brussels, September 2.

Cooper, Richard. 1999. International Approaches to Global Climate Change. Working Paper No. 99-03, Weatherhead Center for International Affairs, Harvard University, January.

———. 2004. A Carbon Tax in China. White Paper, Climate Policy Center, Washington, D.C., August.

Dam, Kenneth W. 2006. China As a Test Case: Is the Rule of Law Essential for Economic Growth? Olin Working Paper No. 275, University of Chicago Law and Economics.

Deutch, John. 2005. What Should the Government Do to Encourage Technical Change in the Energy Sector? Working Paper 0509, Massachusetts Institute of Technology, Center for Energy and Environmental Policy Research.

Dinan, Terry, and David Austin. 2003. Economic Costs of Fuel Economy Standards Versus a Tax on Gasoline. Congressional Budget Office, December. Available at: http://www.cbo.gov/ftpdocs/49xx/doc4917/12-24-03_CAFE.pdf

Dobriansky, Paula. 2005. Remarks to the opening plenary of the eleventh session of the Conference of the Parties (COP 11) to the U.N. Framework Convention on Climate Change (UNFCCC), Montreal, Canada, December 7.

Edmonds, Jae, and Gerry Stokes. 2003. Launching a Technology Revolution. In *Climate Policy for the 21st Century: Meeting the Long-Term Challenge of Global Warming*, ed. David Michel. Washington, D.C.: Center for Transatlantic Relations.

Environmental News Services. 2006. Canada's New Government Cold Shoulders Climate Change Action, April 4, http://www.ens-newswire.com/ens/apr2006/2006-04-04-01.asp (October 4, 2006).

Ermarth, Michael. 1978. *Wilhelm Dilthey: The Critique Of Historical Reason.* Chicago: University of Chicago Press.

Fichthorn, Norman W., and Allison D. Wood. 2005. Constitutional Principles Prohibit States from Regulating CO_2 Emissions. *Legal Backgrounder* 20 (47), http://www.wlf.org/upload/092305 LBFichthorn.pdf (accessed October 5, 2006).

Gallup Organization. 2006a. *American's Perceptions: Environment.* Gallup Poll News Service, March.

Gallup Organization. 2006b. Summary Tabs for Concern About 12 U.S. Domestic Issues—Environment Included. In *American's Perceptions: Environment.* The Gallup Poll, March, 186–91, 321–56.

Green, Chris, Soham Baksi, and Maryam Dilmaghani. 2005. Challenges to a Sustainable Energy Future in a Climate Change Setting. Paper prepared for a Hydrogen & Governance Workshop: Exploring Paths to a Low-Carbon Society. Center for Global Studies and Institute for Integrated Energy Systems, University of Victoria, October 16–18.

Grundig, Frank, Hugh Ward, and Ethan R. Zorick. 2001. Modeling Global Climate Negotiations. In *International Relations and Global Climate Change*, ed. Urs Luderbacher and Detlef F. Sprinz. Cambridge, Mass.: MIT Press.

Hanson, Craig, and James R. Hendricks, Jr. 2006. Taxing Carbon to Finance Tax Reform. Issue brief for Duke Energy and World Resources Institute, Washington, D.C., March.

Heller, Thomas C., and P.R. Shukla, 2003. Development and Climate: Engaging Developing Countries. In *Beyond Kyoto: Advancing the International Effort Against Climate Change.* Published by Pew Center on Global Climate Change. Available at: http://iis-db.stanford.edu/pubs/20860/ Development_ and_Climate.pdf.

Hennessy, Patrick. 2005. Blair Reconsiders Effectiveness of Kyoto. *Washington Times*, September 26.

Hoffert, Martin I., Ken Caldeira, Gregory Benford, David R. Criswell, Christopher Green, Howard Herzog, Atul K. Jain, Haroon S. Kheshgi, Klaus S. Lackner, John S. Lewis, H. Douglas Lightfoot, Wallace Manheimer, John C. Mankins, Michael E. Mauel, L. John Perkins, Michael E. Schlesinger, Tyler Volk, and Tom M. L. Wigley. 2002. Advanced Technology Paths to Global Climate Stability: Energy for a Greenhouse Planet. *Science* 298 (November 1): 981–87.

Homer-Dixon, Thomas F. 2002. Environmental Changes as Causes of Acute Conflict. In *Conflict After the Cold War: Arguments on Causes of War and Peace*, ed. Richard K. Betts. New York: Longman.

Hourcade, Jean-Charles, and Priyadarshi Shukla. 2001. Global, Regional, and National Costs and Ancillary Benefits of Mitigation. In *Climate Change 2001 Mitigation: Contribution of Working Group III to the Third Assessment Report of the Intergovernmental Panel on Climate Change*, ed. B. Metz, O. Davidson, R. Swart, and J. Pan. New York: Cambridge University Press, 2001.

Hubbard, R. Glenn, and Joseph E. Stiglitz. 2003. Letter to Senators John McCain and Joseph Lieberman. Columbia Business School, June 12.

Hunton & Williams. 2006. Governor Schwarzenegger Signs New Climate Change Law—Part of the Emerging National and International Picture. Client Alert from the Climate Change Law and Policy Practice, September 30, http://www.hunton.com/files/tbl_s10News%5 CFile Upload44%5C13457%5CClean_Industry_Initiative_Alert.pdf (accessed October 4, 2006).

Jacoby, Henry D. 2004. Modeling Human-Climate Interaction. In *State of the Planet: Frontiers and Challenges in Geophysics*, ed. R. S. J. Sparks and C. J. Hawksworth. Geophysical Monograph Series, vol. 150. Washington, D.C.: AGU, 307–17.

Japan. Ministry of Economy, Trade and Industry (METI). 2004. Sustainable Future Framework on Climate Change. Interim report, December.

Jones, Bryan D. 2001. *Politics and the Architecture of Choice: Bounded Rationality and Governance*. Chicago: University of Chicago Press.

Joskow, Paul L., and Richard Schmalensee. 1997. The Political Economy of Market-Based Environmental Policy: The U.S. Acid Rain Program. *Journal of Law & Economics* 41 (1): 37–83.

Keeler, Andrew. 2004. An Evaluation of State Carbon Dioxide Reduction Policies. Working paper, Climate Policy Center, Washington, D.C., January.

Keith, David W., and Hadi Dowlatabadi. 1992. A Serious Look at Geoengineering. *Eos, Transactions American Geophysical Union* 73: 289–93.

Kempton, Willett, James S. Boster, and Jennifer A. Hartley. 1999. *Environmental Values in American Culture*. Cambridge, Mass.: MIT Press.

Kingdon, John W. 1995. *Agendas, Alternatives, and Public Policies*. 2nd ed. New York: Longman.

Ladd, Everett Carl, and Karlyn H. Bowman. 1995. *Attitudes Toward the Environment: Twenty-Five Years After Earth Day.* Washington, D.C.: AEI Press.

Lal, Deepak. 1999. *Unfinished Business: India in the World Economy.* Oxford: Oxford University Press.

Leopold, Evelyn. 2004. Annan Lashes at Critics on Iraq Oil, Food Scandal. Reuters, April 28.

Lucas, Caroline. 2005. Blair U-Turn Has Threatened Global Co-operation on Tackling Climate Change. *The Green Party*, http://www.greenparty. org.uk/news/2216 (accessed October 4, 2006).

Mandelbaum, Michael. 2005. *The Case for Goliath: How America Acts As The World's Government In The 21st Century.* New York: Public Affairs.

Marburger, John. 2005. Scientific Integrity in Government (speech). American Physical Society April Meeting, April 17.

Montgomery, W. David, and Anne Smith. 2005. Price, Quantity, and Technology Strategies for Climate Change Policy, CRA International, http://www.wesleyan.edu/econ/seminar/2006s/montgomery.pdf#search=%22. %20Price%2C%20Quantity%2C%20and%20Technology%20Strategies %20for%20Climate%20Change%20Policy%22 (accessed October 4, 2006).

Montgomery, W. David, and Sugandha D. Tuladhar. 2006. The Asia Pacific Partnership: Its Role in Promoting a Positive Climate for Investment, Economic Growth and Greenhouse Gas Reductions. Paper prepared for the International Council for Capital Formation, CRA International, June, http://www.iccfglobal.org/research/climate/index.html (accessed October 5, 2006).

National Academy of Sciences, Committee on Prospering in the Global Economy of the 21st Century: An Agenda for American Science and Technology, National Academy of Engineering, and Institute of Medicine. 2006. *Rising Above the Gathering Storm: Energizing and Employing America for a Brighter Economic Future*, National Academies Press, http://www.nap.edu/catalog/11463.html#toc (accessed October 4, 2006).

National Academy of Sciences, Committee on Science, Engineering, and Public Policy. 1992. *Policy Implications of Greenhouse Warming: Mitigation, Adaptation, and the Science Base*, National Academies Press, http://newton.nap.edu/catalog/1605.html (accessed October 4, 2006).

National Research Council. 2005. *Thinking Strategically: The Appropriate Use of Metrics for the Climate Change Science Program*, National Academies Press, http://www.nap.edu/catalog/11292.html (accessed October 4, 2006).

Newell, Richard G., and Nathan E. Wilson. 2005. Technology Prizes for Climate Change Mitigation. RFF Discussion Paper 05-33, Resources for the Future, Washington, D.C., June.

Nivola, Pietro S., and Robert W. Crandall. 1995. *The Extra Mile: Rethinking Energy Policy for Automotive Transportation*. Washington, D.C.: Brookings Institute Press.

Nordhaus, William D. 2001. Modeling Induced Innovation in Climate Change Policy. Working paper, National Research Council, Yale University.

———. 2004. Economic Modeling of Climate Change: Where Have We Gone? Where Should We Go? Powerpoint presentation at annual climate change conference hosted by the author in Snowmass, Colo., August.

———. 2005. Life After Kyoto: Alternative Approaches To Global Warming Policies. NBER Working Paper 11889, National Bureau of Economic Research, December.

Nordhaus, William D., and Joseph Boyer. 2000. *Warming the World: Economic Models of Global Warming*. Cambridge, Mass.: MIT Press.

Nordhaus, William D., and Zili Yang. 1996. Regional Dynamic General-Equilibrium Model of Alternative. *American Economic Review* 86 (4): 241–65.

North, Douglas C. 1990. *Institutions, Institutional Change and Economic Performance*. Cambridge: Cambridge University Press.

Odom, William E., and Robert Dujarric. 2004. *America's Inadvertent Empire*. New Haven: Yale University Press.

O'Keefe, William. 2006. "'Self-Sufficiency' vs. Economic Reality." *Washington Times*, February 3.

O'Keefe, William, and Jeff Kueter. 2006. *Transportation Fuels from Biomass: An Interesting, But Limited, Option*. Washington, D.C.: George C. Marshall Institute.

Pareto, Vilfredo. 1966. *Sociological Writings*. New York: Frederick A. Praeger.

Pizer, William. 1999. *Choosing Price or Quantity Controls for Greenhouse Gases*. Climate Issue Brief No. 17. Washington D.C.: Resources for the Future, July.

———. 2004. A Tale Of Two Policies. In *Painting The White House Green: Rationalizing Environmental Policy Inside the Executive Office of the President*, ed. Randall Lutter and Jason F. Shogren. Washington, D.C.: Resources for the Future.

Popp, David. 2004. R&D Subsidies and Climate Policy: Is There a "Free Lunch?" NBER Working Paper 10880, National Bureau of Economic Research, Cambridge, Mass., October.

Prinn, Ronald G. 2004. "Complexities in the Climate System and Uncertainties in Forecast." In *State of the Planet: Frontiers and Challenges in Geophysics,* ed. R. S. J. Sparks and C. J. Hawksworth. Geophysical Monograph Series, vol. 150. Washington, D.C.: AGU, 297–305.

Reinstein, Robert A. 2004. A Possible Way Forward on Climate Change. *Mitigation and Adaptation Strategies for Global Change* 9 (3): 245–309.

Reis, Victor H. 1999. Statement for DOE on reorganization of national security programs, http://www.fas.org/irp/congress/1999_hr/99-07-14reis.htm (accessed October 4, 2006).

Samuelson, Robert J. 2006. Global Warming's Real Inconvenient Truth. *Washington Post,* July 5, A13.

Saunders, Paul J., and Vaughan C. Turekian. 2006. Warming to Climate Change. *The National Interest,* no. 84 (summer): 78–84.

Schelling, Thomas C. 2002. What Makes Greenhouse Sense? Time to Rethink the Kyoto Protocol. *Foreign Affairs* 81 (3): 2–9.

———. 2005. What Makes Greenhouse Sense? *Indiana Law Review* 38:581–93.

Smith, Anne. 2006. Emissions Market—Planning for Compliance. Presented at the 2006 Spring Coal Forum of the American Coal Council, Birmingham, Ala., May 24.

Smith, Anne E., Martin T. Ross, and W. David Montgomery. 2002. Implications of Trading Implementation Design for Equity-Efficiency Trade-Offs in Carbon Permit Allocations. Working Paper. Boston: Charles River Associates, December.

Smith, Joel B. 2004. A Synthesis of Potential Climate Change Impacts on the U.S. Report prepared for the Pew Center on Global Climate Change, April.

Stavins, Robert N. 1996. Policy Instruments for Climate Change: How Can National Governments Address a Global Problem? Discussion Paper E-96-03, Kennedy School of Government, Harvard University, December.

Stokes, Donald. 1997. *Pasteur's Quadrant: Basic Science and Technological Innovation.* Washington, D.C.: Brookings Institution.

Szabo, Stephen F. 2004. *Parting Ways: The Crisis In German-American Relations.* Washington, D.C.: Brookings Institution.

Teller, Edward, Roderick Hyde, Muriel Ishikawa, John Nuckolls, and Lowell Wood. 2004. Active Stabilization of Climate: Inexpensive, Low Risk, Near-Term Options for Preventing Global Warming and Ice Ages via Technologically Varied Solar Radiative Forcing. Livermore National Laboratory, University of California Lawrence. Presented at the Tyndall Centre and Cambridge-MIT Institute Symposium on Macro-Engineering

Options for Climate Change Management and Mitigation, Isaac Newton Institute, Cambridge, England, January 7–9.

Thorning, Margo. 2002. Kyoto Protocol and Beyond: Economic Impacts on EU Countries. American Council for Capital Formation, October, http://www.accf.org/pdf/ACCF_KyotoEconImp.pdf (last accessed October 5, 2006).

United Kingdom. Parliament. House of Lords. Select Committee on Economic Affairs. 2005. *The Economics of Climate Change*. HL Paper 12-I (Vol. I: Report). London: The Stationary Office Limited, July.

United Nations Framework Convention on Climate Change (UNFCCC). 2005. National greenhouse gas inventory data for the period 1990–2003 and status reporting (October 12, 2005) http://unfccc.int/resource/docs/2005/sbi/eng/17.pdf (last accessed October 7, 2006).

U.S. Climate Change Technology Program. 2005. *Strategic Plan, Draft for Public Comment*, September, http://www.climatetechnology.gov/strat-plan/draft/index.htm (accessed October 4, 2006).

U.S. State Department. 2006. Briefing on the U.S. Partnership on Clean Development and Climate Change. By Paula Dobriansky and James Connaughton, January 6.

U.S. House of Representatives, Committee on Appropriations. 2006a. *House Report 109-174.* 109th Cong., 2d sess., May 19.

U.S. House of Representatives. Committee on Government Reform. 2006b. Energy and Climate Change Research—DARPA Model. Testimony by Richard van Atta, September 21, 109th Cong., 2nd sess. Available at: http://reform.house.gov/UploadedFiles/ARPA%20E%20testimony%20final%20092106.pdf (last accessed October 8, 2006).

U.S. Senate. 2005. Committee on Environment and Public Works. Testimony by Harlan L. Watson, October 5, 109th Cong., 1st sess., http://www.state.gov/g/oes/rls/rm/54306.htm (accessed October 4, 2006).

U.S. Senate. 2006a. The Role of Science in the Asia-Pacific Partnership. Testimony by James L. Connaughton, April 5, 109th Cong., 2nd sess.

U.S. Senate. 2006b. The Role of Science in the Asia-Pacific Partnership. Testimony by W. David Montgomery, April 5. 109th Cong., 2nd sess.

van Atta, Richard. 2005. Energy and Climate Change Research—DARPA Model. Presented to the Washington Roundtable on Science and Public Policy, National Press Club, Washington, D.C., November.

Wirl, Franz, Claus Huber, and I. O. Walker. 1998. Joint Implementation: Strategic Reactions and Possible Remedies. *Environmental and Resource Economics* 12 (2): 203–224.

Yang, Zili, and Henry D. Jacoby. 1997. *Necessary Conditions for Stabilization Agreements*. Cambridge: MIT Press.

About the Author

Lee Lane has been the executive director of the Climate Policy Center (CPC) since the founding of its predecessor organization in 2000. Mr. Lane leads the development and implementation of the organization's strategic options and directs its overall management. During his tenure as executive director, CPC has expanded its scope to encompass emission control policies, energy R&D, and the search for effective international agreements on climate change.

Recently, Mr. Lane has completed three book chapters on climate policy. The most recent is "Climate Change and Security Policy," to be published in the American University National Security and Law Society's book, *Proceedings from the First Annual Symposium on Emerging Issues in National and International Security*. Another article, "A New Paradigm for U.S. Climate Policy," appears in *Climate Policy for the 21st Century: Meeting the Long-Term Challenge of Global Warming*, published by the Center for Transatlantic Relations of the School of Advanced International Studies of Johns Hopkins University. Mr. Lane is also the author of "The Political Economy of U.S. Greenhouse Gas Controls," which has been published in *Punctuated Equilibrium and the Dynamics of U.S. Environmental Policy* (Yale University Press, spring 2006). Mr. Lane has also authored several climate policy white papers that can be found at CPC's web site, www.CPC-inc.org.

Index